DATE DUE

EARLY
AMERICAN
EMBROIDERY
DESIGNS

BOOKS BY MILDRED J. DAVIS

Early American Embroidery Designs
The Art of Crewel Embroidery

EARLY AMERICAN EMBROIDERY DESIGNS

by MILDRED J. DAVIS

Crown Publishers, Inc.
New York

Dedicated
to
American embroiderers everywhere
who share my
interest in the past,
enthusiasm for the present,
and hopes for the future

ACKNOWLEDGMENTS

Expressions of appreciation for assistance in preparing a book for publication should, if we heed the proverb about charity, start with those at home. It is no exaggeration to say that without the untiring efforts of my husband this book would not be in your hands today. He undertook the formidable task of communicating with museums, historical societies, and individuals all over the country in an effort to locate outstanding colonial embroideries, especially ones which have not heretofore been accorded the recognition due them. As a result, several magnificent pieces are for the first time pictured in a book about American embroideries.

My daughter Patricia actively participated in preparing some of the text and offered valuable suggestions about the written material. My son Wingfield helped more than he knows by freeing me of other responsibilities that I might have occasional periods of uninterrupted quiet to bring all the pieces of this book together.

One of the finest examples of early South Carolina embroideries in this book is due to the interest

and enthusiasm of my cousin, Mary Louise Filipiak, of Florence, South Carolina; she discovered it and secured permission for its inclusion. My sincere appreciation goes to Mr. and Mrs. John W. Campbell of Westfield, New Jersey, who generously gave me access to their own collection of American embroidery pictures. Also to Mrs. Ralph Byer of Chestnut Hill, Massachusetts, for taking pictures of some of the New England pieces, and to Mr. William D. Hood, Jr., of Raleigh, North Carolina, who photographed embroideries in The Valentine Museum.

My great indebtedness is scattered throughout the country to the many museums, historical societies, and individuals without whose generous cooperation this book could never have been completed. To name them all would be to accent the obvious; their captions and credits bespeak their invaluable contributions.

I am particularly grateful to Miss Catherine Fennelly of Old Sturbridge Village, Mrs. Dassah Saulpaugh of the Brooklyn Museum, Miss Alice Beer of The Cooper-Hewitt Museum of Design, and Mrs. Wilber S. King of Pittsburgh, who read portions of the manuscript and made valuable suggestions.

Many others gave freely of their time, their specialized knowledge, their interest, and were immeasurably helpful in many ways: Mrs. Florence Montgomery of the Henry Francis du Pont Winterthur Museum, Miss Edith Standen and Miss Mary Glaze of The Metropolitan Museum of Art, Mr. Frank L. Horton of the Museum of Early Southern Decorative Arts, Mr. Robert B. Mayo and Mrs. Martha T. Boelt of The Valentine Museum, Mrs. Virginia Partridge of the New York State Historical Association, Mrs. Eleanor Duncan and Miss Mildred B. Lanier of Colonial Williamsburg, Miss Imelda G. DeGraw of The Denver Art Museum, Mr. L. Herbert Callister of The Wadsworth Atheneum, Mr. Philip H. Dunbar of The Connecticut Historical Society, Mr. and Mrs. Henry Flynt and Mr. J. Peter Spang III of the Heritage Foundation, Mrs. Anne Cooper, Librarian, Salem College, Mrs. Janis K. Obst of the Minnesota Historical Society, and Mrs. Judson T. Shaplin of the City Art Museum of St. Louis.

Finally, for their part in coordinating a seemingly endless collection of pictures, assorted notes, and manuscript, my concluding appreciation goes to my editor, Helen Sterling, and to Ann Cahn, copy editor and closing link between author and reader.

CONTENTS

PROLOGUE   9

INTRODUCTION   13

I. *Bed Furnishings*   37

COLOR SECTION   65

II. *Apparel and Accessories*   117
III. *Pictorial Needlework*   133

EPILOGUE   151

APPENDIX

   STATE FLOWERS, BIRDS, AND TREES   152

   BIBLIOGRAPHY   154

   INDEX   157

PROLOGUE

The period designated Early American in this book covers some one hundred and thirty-five years, beginning a little before 1700 and ending about 1825.

It was not until the final quarter of the seventeenth century that the colonial population had grown large enough, and secure enough in its foothold upon the Atlantic seaboard, to begin creating its own cultural forms and traditions. It was a slow and uncertain process at first, for the colonists were greatly influenced by the diverse cultural patterns of their European homelands. Gradually, however, designs that were recognizably American in interpretation began to appear in needlework and other decorative art forms, a trend which continued with gathering strength through most of the eighteenth century. Then, early in the 1800's, many of the design ideas created during this period began losing ground to the forces propelling the Industrial Revolution into being, a condition which soon marked the end of early American embroidery development.

The embroidery designs selected as representative of the colonial years were chosen from apparel, household linens, bed hangings, curtains, screens, furniture coverings, and other "stuffs" in contemporary use. They are displayed, with brief descriptions, in three broad groupings: various items of bed furnishings, apparel and household accessories, and pictorial needlework. A major consideration in the selection process was adaptability to the decorative arts in the world of today.

Samplers, which were one of the domestic keystones in the schooling of all genteel young ladies, are limited to a few examples. Memorial pieces, an elegaic conceit of the early 1800's, are apart from the mainstream of decorative embroideries and are also limited. Both have been thoroughly covered in other studies.

Because the emphasis in this book has been placed on design development rather than techniques or materials used, particular types of embroidery such as canvas work or white work, or embroidery done in wool, cotton, silk, and so on, are commented upon only briefly.

The colonists published no books on the needle arts; their newspapers and magazines contained few references which can be used as progressive stepping stones into the past. Thus, with the mystiques of decorative needlework having, for the most part, passed orally from mother to daughter, from teacher to pupil, the tracing of design development involves a substantial degree of enlightened conjecture: enlightened in the sense of being aware of the many forces — economic, social, environmental, cultural, and hereditary — tending to influence design motifs; conjectural in the sense of pairing substantiated evidence with reasonable assumptions, being careful to avoid dogmatic conclusions.

All too frequently names, dates, and places, sometimes all three, are missing on early embroideries, making it difficult, often impossible, to trace chronological or geographical design development. Despite these obstacles, one of the more rewarding aspects of research into the subject of colonial embroideries is the collateral satisfaction derived from a deeper understanding of the times and the people who were creating a unique society upon the American continent.

This book is deeply immersed in traditional designs as must be any study of early American decorative arts. There are those whose preference for modern concepts permits scant enthusiasm for earlier forms. Yet a study of these early motifs is an inescapable prelude to a comprehensive understanding of the whole subject of American embroidery. A surprising number of design ideas which at first glance appear to be new, unique, have roots solidly planted in the past. By the same token, the best of today's concepts will, if they survive, become a part of tomorrow's traditional heritage.

It has been suggested that our civilization is like an endless fabric in which the warp threads represent the stream of continuity from generation to generation, while the weft threads representing the transient forces daily weaving in and out of the lines of continuity, some adding their own color to the fabric, some lost in the ever-lengthening background.

My wish is that in studying the distinctive contributions of early American embroiderers each of us may be encouraged to add her own individual colors to the endless fabric.

MILDRED J. DAVIS

Chestnut Hill, Massachusetts

EARLY
AMERICAN
EMBROIDERY
DESIGNS

Featuring floral and arboreal sprigs, this linen hanging was made in fifth-century Egypt. It was excavated in 1898-1899 in a burying ground near Damietta, lower Egypt. The motifs, forerunners of bouquets and fruit trees used in early American embroideries, are worked in a chain stitch with dark blue, yellow, pink, and three shades of green twisted wools. Border and flowers have shades of red and purple.

Courtesy Victoria and Albert Museum, London

INTRODUCTION

". . . in the course of human events . . ."

Colonial design traditions are treasured natural resources, scions of an honorable ancestry wrought by colonists skilled in the arts of the Old World: carpenters, shipwrights, cabinetmakers, silversmiths, artists, engravers and printers, carvers, weavers, potters, glass and ornamental metalworkers, embroiderers, and others. These artisans adapted their skills to colonial needs and limitations, trained apprentices in the essential disciplines, and were soon making indelible impressions upon their new homeland.

Of all the decorative arts, embroidery was perhaps unique. Unlike cabinetmaking, engraving, silversmithing, and other crafts almost wholly dominated by men, it was almost completely expressive of women's tastes and skills. It involved more people in creative roles. A relatively small percentage of the population built furniture, became artists, or cut wood blocks for printing, but nearly every woman, no matter how humble her station, could manage to make at least a few embroideries. Needlework offered greater latitude in creative invention. Household accessories made by colonial craftsmen were, for the most part, tied by a fairly short leash to fashions then a la mode; embroidery could be as expressive of the maker's individuality as she wished.

It was a significant coincidence that the Early American era was the chronological cousin to the Age of Enlightenment, which sparkled through one of the liveliest and most fascinating centuries in the history of our ancestors.

The two periods began continents apart in essence as well as in fact. The Age of Enlightenment was born in Europe and was nurtured by its philosophers, statesmen, scientists, writers, artists, musicians, and craftsmen, all of whom profoundly influenced the economic, political, and cultural development of the American colonies.

Colonial America was an interested spectator on the edge of the intellectual and political ferments of Europe until it took center stage with its own epic drama in 1775. When clash of arms followed clash of ideas, the land and its people were ravaged for seven long years until the new nation won independence.

Little of these momentous events was reflected in contemporary embroidery motifs. Quieter influences prevailed within the home, where woman's need of beauty, serenity, and a family secure within the sphere of her love and understanding sought and found fulfillment.

European society of the Enlightenment was by no means exclusively concerned with intellectual pursuits. Far from it. The cultivation of pleasure became a fine art. Elegance in every form was pursued avidly, creating in its wake craftsmen whose consummate skills have seldom been equaled.

For many years colonial America had little time or means for embracing either the intellectual or social preoccupations of Europe. A people busily engaged in hewing a country out of a wilderness had plenty of other concerns to put first. During much of the seventeenth century, many colonial homes were family shelters in a unique sense: houses built to ward off invaders. As imminent danger of attack receded into the background, security precautions were gradually discarded, thus opening the way for important architectural improvements. Shutters were removed, windows and doorways enlarged, and ornamental detail added. Interiors became more spacious, the possibilities for comfortable living were greatly expanded, and proper furnishing and decoration became the subject of growing interest and concern.

Economic growth accompanied these changes: trade and agriculture became increasingly important. The foundations for a substantial middle class were laid, thus bringing more and more colonists into the eighteenth century who were prepared to embrace the esthetic transformation then beginning in Europe. When economic development advanced to the point of sustaining a society encompassing middle- and upper-income classes, the pursuit of luxury was reaching flood tide abroad. Inevitably some of this passion for the newest and most fashionable concomitants to pleasant living began to overflow into colonial America.

Improvements in the economic and social milieu not only stimulated import trade, they gave impetus to the growth of the decorative arts within the colonies. Craftsmen everywhere responded to expanding opportunities. Each contributed, in varying degrees, to the development of household accessories displaying simple good taste in line, form, and decoration, and the inherent honesty of careful workmanship. Collectively, colonial men and women merged their talents into a decorative idiom that still evokes deep-seated emotional and intellectual responses more than two centuries later.

Two widely different influences played important roles in shaping early American embroidery designs. One originated abroad and was freshly reinforced by nearly every ship bringing settlers, merchandise, books, and periodicals into the colonies: the exquisite designs created by the master craftsmen of Europe. The other was born of, nurtured and conditioned by local necessity: having to make do with what was available.

The final decades of the seventeenth century witnessed the peak of European interest in lavishly executed embroideries characterized by densely elaborate motifs. Early in the eighteenth century these ornate patterns gradually began giving way to designs in which spaciousness and subtlety of treatment became the dominant style, *joie de vivre* the dominant emotion. Silk became the important medium, and with its use came a greater delicacy of line and finesse in shading techniques. In this transition the French had no peers; their superiority was recognized throughout the Western world.

In Europe these changes came about in the course of an esthetic evolution; in America simplicity of design was also the result of practical necessity. Fabrics and yarns were scarce, expensive when they could be bought, and demanding of much time and effort when created in the home. Happily, many of the patterns created by the harsh realities of a frontier society blended harmoniously with those fashioned in the cultural centers of Europe, thus establishing an esthetic kinship of the most improbable parentage.

England, of course, was the major funnel

through which European decorative influences reached the colonies. The English were influenced by the creative genius and skills of Continental craftsmen, especially those of France, and all of Europe responded to decorative motifs brought from exotic lands by its far-ranging seafarers. Designs bearing the imprint of Near and Far Eastern cultures were particularly stimulating.

Much has been conjectured about the origins of colonial designs. Little supporting documentation exists so the subject remains deep in the realm of speculation. Logically, there were four general source categories: design traditions from the homelands of settlers born abroad; imported design ideas from a variety of sources — printed embroidery patterns, painted and printed fabrics, wallpapers, decorated household accessories, finished embroideries created abroad; schools and independent teachers in the colonies; inspirations derived from the fascinating, and sometimes forbidding, new world surrounding the colonists.

Tracing the paths taken by incoming colonists adds an interesting dimension to the study of design evolution. Normally, newcomers were members of national groups who frequently settled in the same general areas. The common bonds of national identity and shared language and traditions were powerful adhesives when confronting the uncertainties of a strange land.

The Spanish, English, Dutch, and Swedes were the first to plant colonies here. The Spanish settled on the east coast of Florida, founding St. Augustine, oldest city in the United States, in the late sixteenth century. There they remained until early in the eighteenth century, when they undertook limited expansion into the coastal regions of Louisiana and Mississippi. The English, Dutch, and Swedes created their first settlements early in the seventeenth century, the Dutch settling mostly along the Hudson Valley, the Swedes along the Delaware Valley, the English in Virginia and New England.

French Huguenots and Germans were next, beginning late in the seventeenth century. The Huguenots favored South Carolina, Pennsylvania,

New York, and Virginia. Other French began arriving about forty years later, many of them going to Louisiana, where, around mid-century, their numbers were augmented by a considerable group of Acadians deported from Nova Scotia by the British. The Germans first concentrated in southeastern Pennsylvania, later expanding into Delaware and Maryland, and eventually penetrating the back-country areas of Virginia and the Carolinas via the Shenandoah Valley. A few Germans also came into the country through South Carolina.

Scots and Scotch-Irish (Scots who first sought refuge in Ulster and from there migrated to the colonies) began arriving in significant numbers in the first quarter of the eighteenth century, Philadelphia and Charleston being the chief ports of entry. Most of them immediately pushed on to the frontiers of Pennsylvania, Maryland, Virginia, and the Carolinas. Others migrated to northern New England, especially sections of New Hampshire.

The earliest comprehensive population figures, those of the first Federal census (1790), show national origins of residents with European backgrounds as 61 percent English, about 19 percent Scotch, Irish, and Welsh, 9 percent German, 3 percent Dutch, and 2 percent French, with the remaining 6 percent covering all other European nationalities.

The English, Scots, Irish, and Welsh shared the same design traditions, predominantly those of England. The French, Germans, Spanish, Swedes, and a scattering of other nationalities, each in varying degrees contributed to our colonial heritage from their homeland traditions. Only the Dutch along the Hudson Valley and the Germans, popularly known as Pennsylvania Dutch, preserved their own decorative motifs from almost complete absorption into colonial design conventions. These sturdy, energetic people built compact self-contained communities, and, behind the barriers of their native languages, made a determined effort to preserve their cultural values intact.

Popular contributions of the other ethnic groups were adopted into colonial designs, sometimes with little or no variation, sometimes with modifi-

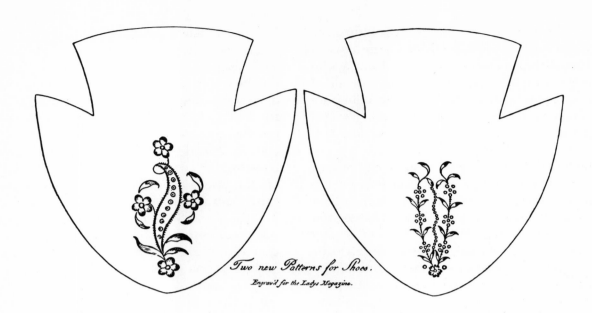

Two new Patterns for Shoes.

Engrav'd for the Lady's Magazine.

Colonial embroiderers were offered patterns for shoes and sprigs in the pages of *The Lady's Magazine* in 1776. Published in London, it also circulated in America.

Courtesy Victoria and Albert Museum, London

New Patterns of Sprigs.   *Engrav'd for the Lady's Magazine.*

cations to accommodate personal fancies. Patterns with pronounced characteristics directly associated with specific European countries were in all likelihood developed abroad and brought to America, although it is possible that some were created here by newly arrived settlers still clinging to homeland traditions. However, it can be assumed with reasonable assurance that designs which only hint at European influence were probably of colonial origin, although in the absence of positive identification on the pieces themselves, or documented histories, authentication is quite difficult.

Emigrating to colonial America must have been a wrenching or exhilarating experience — perhaps a little of both — coupled with apprehensions for the future. Leaving their native lands meant severing ties with familiar places, persons, and things, and took a special kind of determination and courage. To ease the transition from one world to another most settlers brought along as many of their possessions as possible, usually a woefully small collection of the most necessary things, for there was little enough room in the tiny ships. Only memories of their homelands and their dreams for the future could be brought in unstinted quantity.

By the final quarter of the seventeenth century, second and third generations were well launched without ties to Europe anchored by personal association. It was from this point on in colonial development that embroidery designs evidencing inspirations springing from the land itself can be said to have had their tentative beginnings.

The colonists displayed remarkable ingenuity and skill in adapting various Old World implements to their own special needs and, in the process, made them as simple as possible. Of necessity their concerns had to place utility first, with decorative effects added when and if time and materials permitted. Simplification of form went hand in hand with clarity of design.

As it was with implements, so it was with needlework and the other decorative arts. The colonists took the best of the designs which came to hand, refined them to their own needs and capacities, and in so doing helped set the stage for the simplified artistic traditions which have had such a pro-found influence upon the development of the arts in America.

Colonial society on the whole was a body of people who, in a very real sense, were "on the make." They were industriously developing a productive land, creating homes and families, fashioning physical and economic security, evolving a political philosophy with dynamic potential for a world then too preoccupied with its own affairs to pay overmuch attention to this new nation in the making.

Dress became a matter of serious concern to both men and women. It was important that apparel be of a quality and style commensurate with their station in life (perhaps, upon occasion, even venturing to anticipate tomorrow's successes). There was great awareness of fashion, evidenced by repeated references in newspaper advertisements to workmanship in the "newest fashion" and to goods "newly arrived from London." The vast expanse of distance and time between Europe and the colonies bred an avid interest in the very latest word from abroad.

From an amalgam of diverse European peoples inhabiting the colonies certain characteristics shaped by similar economic, social, and political environments and ambitions gradually began to merge into distinctively colonial American patterns of beliefs and conduct. This was nowhere more evident than in the burgeoning middle and leisured classes — the families of skilled craftsmen, shopkeepers, merchants and tradesmen, shipbuilders, mariners, artisans, professional men, provincial officials, landowners. It was this stratum of society which developed and executed many of the designs that have survived to become known as early American. Most of these people lived in or near the thriving seaports, the mainsprings of economic and cultural growth. Here lay ready access to ideas and materials newly imported from Europe. Here too were offered the best educational opportunities for their children.

All during the colonial period most of the inhabitants were scattered along the Atlantic coastal plain where many of them lived in close contact with the sea. Even those who were not within sight or sound of the shore could hardly have been unaware of the vast importance of the ocean and coastal rivers as avenues of commerce vital to the economic life of the colonies, linking them to Europe and to each other. Yet, in spite of their overwhelming importance, there are very few embroideries with ships or other motifs suggesting nautical associations. Perhaps colonial women felt more at ease using designs with which they had direct personal associations — backyard flowers, vines, trees, familiar animals.

Gentility became a much sought social distinction, a quest spurred by the double prongs of desire for local esteem and by the realization that Europe's regard for colonial social graces was at best patronizing when it was not downright derisive.

Individuals offering services for hire — decorative craftsmen, teachers, and others — recognized the appeal of cultural splendor by association and gave assurances in public announcements that their services would be performed in the "genteelest" or the "neatest and most fashionable" and occasionally in the "most elegant manner." A teacher who could infuse her pupils with cultural virtues was a prized community asset; a room decorated in the genteelest manner cloaked those in it with its own aura of elegance. To surround themselves with the drapery of gentility was to partake of it; what was not theirs by gentle birth might become theirs by absorption.

Woman's position in the social order was hedged about by all manner of conventions, admonitions, prohibitions, entreaties, and so on (which women no less than men helped perpetuate). Prescribed were all the virtues calculated to make women more desirable: modesty and goodness, described as "nature's best ornaments," industry, chastity, piety, generosity, affability, unfailing dignity, to name but a few. Proscriptions in similar detail covered those undesirable attributes thought to render the fair sex less enchanting.

Men tended to shy away from women of wit whose learning equaled or, heaven forfend, surpassed their own, especially those whose activities were tainted by intellectual accomplishments. Anne Bradstreet (c. 1612 - 1672), the first colonial poet of any note, progenitor of several distin-

guished American men of letters, spoke for all when she wrote:

I am obnoxious to each carping tongue
  Who says my hand a needle better fits,
A poets pen all scorn I should thus wrong,
  For such despite they cast on female wits:
If what I do prove well, it won't advance,
  They'l say it's stoln, or else it was by chance.

Despite women's carefully defined roles in the social structure they were sometimes called upon to accept responsibilities in what was regarded as man's domain — managing a business, be it shop, manufactory, or plantation. In households where husbands were often away for long periods, or were preoccupied by affairs of state, the women frequently had to become adept at account-keeping, supervising employees, attending the day-to-day minutiae of business affairs, a remarkable achievement considering the limited educational facilities available to them.

Early American embroidery patterns fall into two major groups: adaptations from designs originating in Europe, and original designs created by individual needlewomen.

Embroideries embodying design ideas from abroad were generally popular. The colonists were bound to Europe economically, emotionally, and culturally, and were avid for news and views of the latest fashions created there. When working with design ideas from abroad, local needlewomen could feel reasonably secure from critical comment by fashion-conscious neighbors, and at the same time be spared the necessity of inventing or improvising their own patterns. They might occasionally substitute local flora or fauna for those in the original, but the most likely change, if there was any at all, would be "expanding" the design to cover a larger area. Spacious treatment was especially appropriate to colonial America, where many colonists could look out upon great unsettled areas of open country. It also fitted the "make-do" technique enforced by chronic material shortages.

Design motifs having their roots in the land

itself were drawn by needlewomen more imaginative than most, whose creative impulses were not satisfied with the conventional patterns then in vogue. People everywhere were close to nature, a kinship evident in many of their embroideries. Even those who lived in the largest towns were never far from open country. Wild game and flowers abounded with ample cover for each. Birds, some of whom are now rarely seen or heard in our cities, were familiar to everyone wherever they lived. Man and nature enjoyed a rapport long since forfeited to material achievement.

Some of this rapport undoubtedly wore a bit thin during the cold months. Winter was a long, dreary season to be endured in houses cold and drafty. The kitchen was usually the only room kept warm all day. That and the bed, with its heavy insulating hangings, were the two chief refuges for snug warmth. Churches as a rule were unheated; schools usually had fireplaces which warmed only those within the inner semicircle nearest it. It is not surprising that few early embroideries pictured winter scenes. One may reasonably assume that women working on embroideries during the winter months were remembering summers past or anticipating those to come.

Whatever the design sources, nearly all colonial embroideries shared a basic simplicity in arrangement and execution. Embroidery materials were not available in sufficient supply to permit lavish use, and the relatively unsophisticated colonial society, despite its intense interest in affairs a la mode, was more closely attuned to the simple homely virtues than to the frivolities of Europe.

To assess the degree to which embroideries were inspired by the flora and fauna of the New World is not easy. Many of the most popular flowers, birds, and animals (including those enshrined in folklore) were familiar sights on both sides of the Atlantic. However, it is not always possible to identify which particular flowers or birds were being depicted. Lack of pictorial skills, or perhaps a tendency to endow flowers with hues not found in nature, makes it difficult at times to discern what the embroiderer had in mind. Pictorial skills were seldom equal to the task of distinguishing between birds of similar contour or coloring. Squirrels, rabbits, deer, and horses, are almost always recognizable as such, but there is no way to distinguish between American and European varieties. Aside from an occasional turkey, animals unique to America, such as the raccoon, were seldom pictured.

Design ideas could have come from many everyday sources—a favorite flowering shrub, the first crocus, a honeysuckle-clad fence, fruit trees in full blossom, brilliant-hued butterflies speckling a garden, children at play, birds in a familiar tree, wild geese winging overhead, ducks on a pond, grasshoppers idling the summer away, small forest animals scurrying about their favorite haunts, bees industriously gathering nectar, a village street, the village green lying quiet in the sunlight, an elegant coach-and-four, marching soldiers, frisking lambs, a mare and her colt, a hunter and his dog, fleeting glimpses of deer in the woods—the list is endless.

Many of the early pieces were amazingly well conceived and executed. Some were ambitious beyond the capabilities of their creators. Many designs displayed simplicity of concept neatly complementing simplicity of execution. Others can only be called "primitives." Surviving embroideries had some inherent appeal compelling succeeding generations to preserve them — simple excellence of line and technique perhaps, or certain naïve charms that evoked emotional responses in those who saw them.

Design characteristics are not the only clues to the origins of early embroideries. Background fabrics, threads, yarns, and stitch techniques tell their own stories. Homespun background strongly suggests colonial origin, as do stitches laid for maximum effect using the least amount of thread. However, imported linens, twills, broadcloths, and other fabrics were available to those who could afford them, so the fact of background material other than homespun does not rule out colonial origin. A pattern worked in surface stitches on homespun signifies only that the execution was in the colonial *tradition*; it does not guarantee colonial origin.

Embroidered pictures and bed hangings, imported rugs, tiles, and china complemented the simple, sturdy lines of paneling and furniture in colonial interiors such as this restored Benkard memorial bedroom of 1740 - 1750.

Courtesy Museum of the City of New York

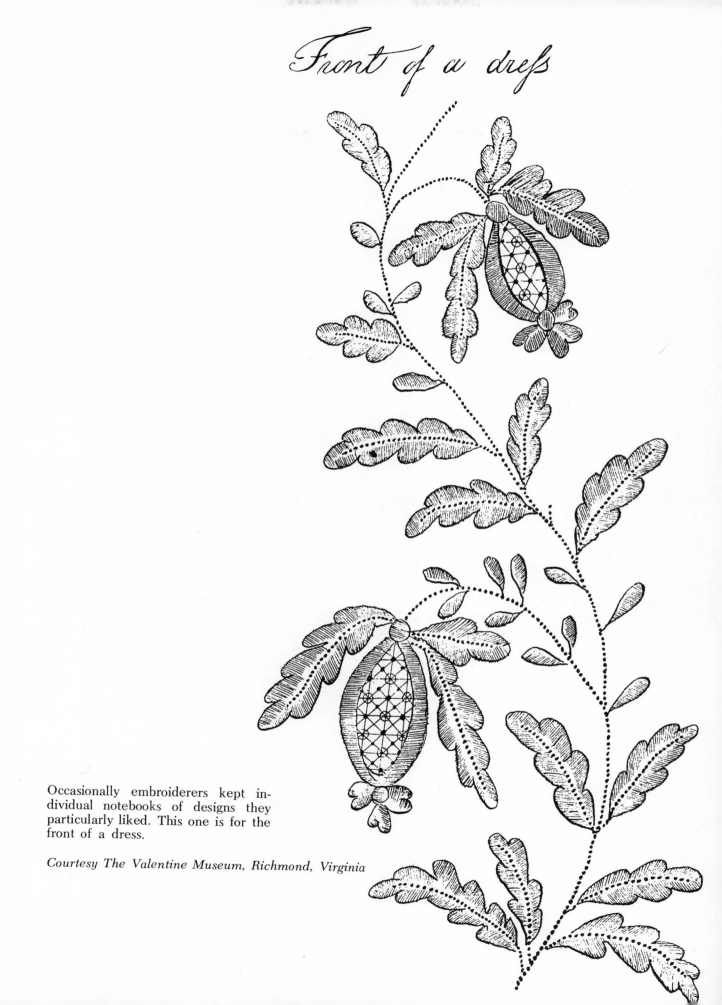

Front of a dress

Occasionally embroiderers kept individual notebooks of designs they particularly liked. This one is for the front of a dress.

Courtesy The Valentine Museum, Richmond, Virginia

Threads available to the colonists included silk, linen, wool, and cotton. For some years, cultivation of silk in the colonies was tried, but with so little success, the idea was eventually abandoned. Attempts to grow flax fared considerably better; indeed, it was one of the staple fibers of the early colonists, who spun it into thread and wove it into cloth, generally called homespun. With the invention of the cotton gin in 1794, the use of flax declined, cotton being more economical to produce. By 1825 large-scale cultivation of flax and manufacture of linen had about run its course in this country.

Cotton and wool were by far the most popular threads for embroidering. Silk was little used, being an imported product, expensive and difficult to obtain. Some linen thread was used but it never attained wide popularity. Wool was generally preferred in the middle and northern colonies, cotton in the southern colonies. An interesting point about the use of cotton thread by southern needle-women was the weight of some of it, occasionally being heavy enough for it to be called twine or small cord. Perhaps one of its appeals lay in the fact that it worked up faster than regular-weight thread. When handled skillfully, it was quite effective.

Many coverlets were made with white thread on a white background. Blue and rose thread was a popular combination throughout the colonies. Blue embroidery on a white background was also popular, and remains a favorite to this day. Examples of these and other favored color combinations may be seen in the color section of this book.

In fairness to our colonial forebears it should be noted that time has undoubtedly dimmed examples of their skills in color handling by all too frequently fading colors to a pale representation of their original hues. The well-preserved pieces to be seen in museums, historical societies, and private collections do attest that the colonists did remarkably well with the coloring materials and techniques available to them.

Many diverse factors in the colonial environment influenced early embroidery designs: textiles, wallpapers, pattern books, illustrated garden books, samplers, schools and independent teachers, portraitists and itinerant artists, and so on. Their influence on design evolution varied from place to place, and from time to time, thus offering many interesting opportunities for further research into this complex subject. The more important of these factors are summarized on the following pages.

Samplers.

The universal popularity of samplers suggests that printed patterns were in limited use during most of the colonial period. Whereas few original patterns have withstood the ravages of use and time, thousands of samplers have survived.

The word "sampler" was a popularization of "exemplar," a pattern or model to be copied from. Samplers originally served as convenient repositories in which various stitches and motifs could be recorded for future reference. Later they became a fashionable form of needlework for adults, as well as an almost universal form of exercise for beginners.

The quality of needlework on existing seventeenth-century samplers suggests that few of them were made by children. It was not until the eighteenth century that samplers with stylized alphabetical and numerical notations became household accessories to the domestic education of all properly reared young ladies.

By the middle of the eighteenth century, sampler motifs displayed much more originality, and the alphabet was reduced to a subordinate position when it appeared at all. Pastoral scenes, enriched by youthful imagination unfettered by rules of perspective, were popular. In general, children's samplers appear to have been more spontaneous reflections of contemporary events, scenes, and emotions than adult embroideries of the same period.

The inclusion of pious verses attained widespread acceptance during the final quarter of the eighteenth century and continued in vogue until sampler-making fell into disfavor about fifty years later. The subjects most often selected were scriptural quotations, meditations upon life and death, and poetic contemplations of feminine virtues:

The best school for a good life, is the
frequent meditation upon a happy death.

MARION RUTHVEN, Aged 7, 1803

To lead the tender mind to virtue's bower,
Pluck the weed & cultivate the flower.

MARTHA PUTNAM, 1797

An exception to the fragile sentiments usually expressed was this forthright declaration in 1800 by a young lady:

Patty Polk did this and she hated every stitch she did in it. She loves to read much more.

Sampler-making was essentially a foundation stone in the learning process and, as such, exercised limited influence on embroidery designs. Even so, samplers are well worth studying for they often tell interesting stories about the community at large as seen through the eyes of its children. There is little doubt that samplers collectively reflect much of the decorative sentiment, and express the mores of the world in which their youthful makers lived. They spanned the whole of the Early American period and (because nearly all of them were dated) are the one form of colonial embroideries in which it is possible to trace a definite chronological pattern of development. Understanding them and what they tell about the environment in which colonial children were reared helps us better understand the world of their parents.

Schools and Teachers.

Throughout the colonial era it was generally considered sufficient that girls be well schooled in the domestic arts and social graces. In most communities a working acquaintance with reading and writing was accounted desirable but cultivation of the feminine "virtues" was paramount.

Teaching the young was an individual family responsibility. Small children learned the rudiments of spelling, reading, writing, and perhaps simple needlework for the girls, at the hands of parents, tutors, or in dame schools usually kept by widows or spinsters. Teachers faced with discipline problems in crowded one-room schools often improvised activities to keep idle hands busy. According to one contemporary pupil, children were put to "shelling peas and other improving occupations" after their toilsome bouts with spelling and reading were done for the day.

Girls taught at home or at dame schools until about the age of eight or ten learned the fundamentals of sewing, and learned to work simple embroidery designs, usually samplers. For many, this ended their formal education, although learning-by-doing continued as they helped with the multitude of household chores that were part and parcel of colonial family living.

Young ladies whose parents could afford it went on to boarding or finishing schools where, typically, they might be offered "Reading, Writing, and English Grammar, Tambour, the agreeable Art of Embroidery, all kinds of Needlework, Millinery, making Gloves and making Lace, Net Work, and weaving Fringes, drawing flowers, Painting, Shell Work, Dancing and Playing the Guitar, with particular attention to morals and manners."

The art of drawing was accounted a most elegant accomplishment and much attention was given to it. Any proficiency in drawing and painting, however modest, would be helpful in laying out embroidery designs.

In some areas, especially the rural South, resident tutors were sometimes engaged to instruct the children of a plantation family, with neighboring children occasionally invited to join them. Usually tutors were young men who taught the three R's, introduced their charges to the classics, and by precept and example sought to inculcate a proper regard for good manners and morals. They rarely dipped into the mystiques of needlework, nor were they expected to, but such talents as they did possess were not allowed to lie fallow as witness these entries in the diary of Philip Fithian, tutor to the sons and daughters of Colonel and Mrs. Carter of Nomini Hall, Virginia:

Tuesday, Dec. 28, 1773 — Evening at Miss

The paper pattern for this petticoat or dress border of 1810-1830 was drawn in indelible ink.

Courtesy Henry Francis du Pont Winterthur Museum

This set of three paper bed valances, American, 1750-1800, was probably made in imitation of embroidered valances.

Courtesy Henry Francis du Pont Winterthur Museum

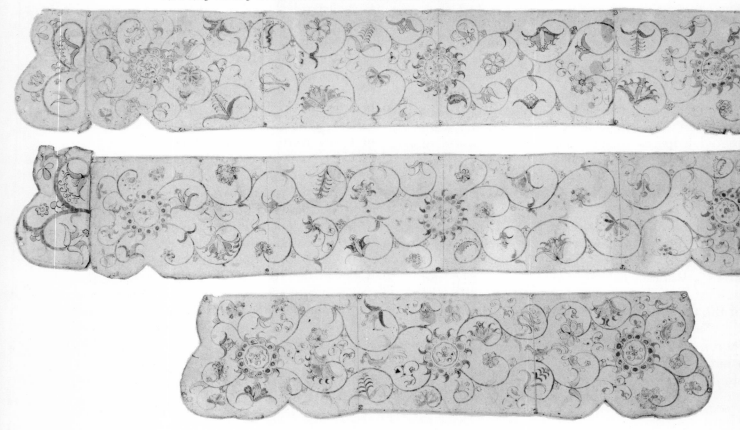

Prissy's Request I drew for her some Flowers on Linen which she is going to embroider, for a various Counterpane.

Wednesday, Dec. 29, 1773 — I drew, this afternoon more Flowers for Miss Prissy.

Needlework instruction in most schools embraced various branches of embroidery, with sampler-making on a somewhat more imaginative level continuing in favor during the latter half of the eighteenth century. Many samplers made during this period reflected the interests and enthusiasms of the young needlewomen who, drawing upon their own intimate worlds for ideas, recorded with youthful naïveté the things and places they best knew and loved. While these ventures into originality had small impact on contemporary embroideries they did encourage an imaginative approach to needlework on the part of the generation then nearing adulthood.

A few of the more fortunate daughters were schooled abroad. One such was Martha Jefferson, daughter of Thomas Jefferson, who accompanied her father to France when he became envoy to the court of Louis XVI. An exchange of notes between Patsy, as she was called, and her father concerns, in part, their opinions on the value of needlework. Patsy, attending a school in Paris in 1787, wrote to her father:

I go slowly with my Livy, it being in such ancient Italian that I cannot read it without my master, and very little even with him.

His parental admonitions were not long in coming forth:

I do not like your saying that you are unable to read the ancient print of your Livy but with the aid of your master. We are always equal to what we undertake with resolution. A little degree of this will enable you to decipher your Livy. If you always lean on your master, you will never be able to proceed without him. It is a part of the American character to consider nothing as desperate; to surmount every difficulty by resolution and contrivance.

In Europe there are shops for every want; its inhabitants, therefore, have no idea that their wants can be supplied otherwise. Remote from all other aid, we are obliged to invent and to execute; to find means within ourselves, and not lean on others. Consider, therefore, the conquering your Livy as an exercise in the habit of surmounting difficulties; a habit which will be necessary to you in the country where you are to live, and without which you will be thought a very helpless animal, and less esteemed. Music, drawing, books, invention, and exercise, will be so many resources to you against ennui. But there are others which, to this object, add that of utility. These are the needle and domestic economy. The latter you can not learn here, but the former you may. In the country life of America there are many moments when a woman can have recourse to nothing but her needle for employment. In a dull company, and in dull weather, for instance, it is ill-manners to read, it is ill-manners to leave them; no card-playing there among genteel people—that is abandoned to blackguards. The needle is then a valuable resource. Besides without knowing how to use it herself, how can the mistress of a family direct the work of her servants?

Patsy got in the last word on needlework:

As for needlework, the only kind that I could learn here would be embroidery, indeed netting also; but I could not do much of those in America, because of the impossibility of having proper silks; however they will not be totally useless.

Many young ladies "curious with the needle" who were schooled abroad naturally absorbed the newest fashions in decorative needlework and, one suspects, may have returned home displaying a slightly patronizing air of Continental sophistication. In any event, they were certainly envied by their stay-at-home contemporaries eager for the latest news of the fashions captivating London and the Continent.

With rare exceptions, school curricula followed

the educational dicta of the day, with emphasis upon social and domestic accomplishments, plus enough instruction in reading and writing to allow for the attainment of a modest degree of literacy.

Teachers and schools were indispensable to the orderly development of design evolution, for in them reposed the disciplined skills that preserved techniques perfected during the years, that marshaled order, form, and continuity out of random inspirations. Although educational facilities in the decorative arts were uneven in geographical distribution, erratic in quantity and quality of instruction, woefully inadequate by nearly every modern criterion, yet, within the context of the society being served, they responded adequately to the demands of the times.

Published Patterns.

There is no record of pattern books being published in colonial America. In fact, they seem to have been in little demand during the eighteenth century, either here or abroad. However, some individual notebooks were compiled by those who wished to preserve various design ideas. A pattern from an exceptionally fine collection in the Valentine Museum, Richmond, Virginia, has been reproduced here.

Although published pattern books were seldom used during the colonial period, individual patterns were printed abroad (usually from copperplate engravings) and were generally available to the public in the larger cities. One source was *The Lady's Magazine,* published in London and popular in the colonies. Beginning in 1774 and continuing for some years thereafter, this periodical offered its readers a needlework pattern nearly every month. No explanatory text accompanied the designs; evidently the ladies were expected to proceed on their own initiative.

Contemporary references to patterns are found in newspaper announcements:

To be had at Mrs. Condy's near Old North Meeting House; All sorts of beautiful Figures on Canvas, for Tent Stick; the Patterns from London, but drawn by her much Cheaper than the English drawing; All sorts of Canvas, without drawing; also Silk Shades, Slacks, Floss, Cruells of all Sorts, the best White Chappel Needles, and every thing for all Sorts of Work.

Boston, *News-Letter,* April, 1743

To be sold by William Trickett, Stationer. . . . Drawings for all kinds of needle work.
Pennsylvania Evening Post, March, 1778

Few original patterns have survived. Their life expectancy was short, due in large measure to the method of transferring patterns to fabrics — piercing holes along the lines of the design through which the pattern was "pounced" onto the ground. Under this sort of usage they usually fell apart.

In addition to pattern notebooks and commercially printed patterns, design ideas came from books illustrated with drawings of plants, flowers, trees, shrubs — garden books, encyclopedias, herbals, and similar publications. Books on calligraphy, many of which included beautiful designs of birds, flowers, and animals, provided another source of design ideas which could be adapted to embroideries. Under the circumstances, it is not surprising there was a considerable degree of similarity in design motifs favored throughout the colonies.

Occasionally, there are examples of line by line duplication of whole designs, such as a petticoat border in the collection of the Museum of Fine Arts, Boston, which, in reduced scale, is duplicated on the apron of a doll now among the exhibits of Colonial Williamsburg.

Printed patterns preserved in museums, libraries, and private collections are nearly all concerned with the decoration of women's costume — aprons, gowns, caps, shoes, handkerchiefs, pockets and pocketbooks, workbags and baskets, petticoats, waistcoats, jackets, flounces, muffs, scarves, and so on. Embroidery was essentially regarded as a feminine accomplishment — although a few professional embroiderers were men — so it is not surprising that pattern-makers catered to the universal desire on the part of women to make their persons and households more attractive.

This embroidery pattern, drawn on parchment, was probably made in New England before 1720.

There is little evidence that commercial patterns were available for large pieces such as coverlets. Existing bed hangings, curtains, valances, and so on, suggest their border designs were often formed by repeating various individual motifs, or sequences of motifs. With the borders taken care of, the center portions could be completed with sprigs or sprays of flowers, or other motifs according to the designer's fancy.

Colonial Magazines.

The first magazines were published in January, 1741. Others followed in fairly steady succession during the remainder of the eighteenth century, all of them short-lived. These early periodicals were much preoccupied with political writings, essays on morality, philosophy, education, advice to young ladies, "physick," comment on social manners and customs, poetry, fiction, and other topics of current interest including meteorological observations. There was little or nothing about the decorative arts. Domestic accomplishments were regarded as entirely women's province and therefore had no proper place in periodicals edited largely by men for men.

There was an overabundance of advice thrust at women, and very little written for them until after the Revolution, when several magazines acknowledged their past derelictions accompanied by promises to make amends. In the words of one: "The fair sex merits our highest attention. If their taste has not hitherto been consulted, or the delicacy of their fancy gratified, we flatter ourselves that the succeeding numbers will make compensation for the former negligence."

Despite such extravagant protestations, the decorative arts continued to receive short shrift until the advent of *Lady's Book*, a monthly publication which later became *Godey's Lady's Book*. Here a small beginning was made in July, 1830, with an article on embroidery which began:

Numerous as are the subjects treated in this work, there are few which furnish a more pleasing occupation than Embroidery. To this art our readers are indebted for some of the most elegant articles of dress. It may, also, afford them opportunities of displaying their taste and ingenuity; and offers a graceful occupation, and an inexhaustable source of laudable and innocent amusement.

Following a short history of embroidery, a greatly reduced pattern for embroidering the cape of a dress was offered, with instructions for tacking the pattern upon the fabric. No suggestions were offered as to stitches or colors. Enlarging the drawing to usable size was left to the ingenuity of the reader. Succeeding issues featured articles on embroidery, but this series was discontinued after only six months. Thereafter, for a short time, five or six patterns a year were shown, without explanatory text, and each devoted to "Embroidery for Head Dresses." It seems apparent that embroidery as a magazine feature was not a compelling topic.

Colonial Newspapers.

The decorative arts fared as poorly in colonial newspapers as in magazines, except in the advertising columns, which provide, for those interested in the early American scene, an invaluable catalogue of the various goods and services available.

The first colonial newspaper, *Publick Occurrences Both Forreign and Domestick*, was published in September, 1690, and immediately suppressed on the grounds it was started "without the least Privity or Countanance of Authority." Fourteen years elapsed before another attempt at newspaper publishing was made. The first successful one was established in 1704, the second in 1719. By 1736, the colonies had a total of eleven active weeklies published in Boston, New York, Philadelphia, Charleston, and Williamsburg.

Patterned Fabrics.

The list of imported textiles offered for sale through newspaper advertisements was quite impressive and included materials in which designs were woven into the fabric, painted or printed upon them.

Damasks and brocades displayed woven designs, with brocades, described as "embroidery made with a loom," offering a greater range of inspirational possibilities. Damask patterns were usually flat, monochromatic, with large-figured continuous patterns, sometimes complex, but more often relatively simple. Brocade patterns, featuring smaller detached figures in relief, tended to be more elaborate, and frequently had polychromatic color schemes.

By far the most likely contributors to those seeking embroidery design ideas were painted or printed fabrics, with their lively, imaginative floral and arboreal designs on silk, linen, and especially cotton grounds. They, more closely than any other figured textiles, were akin to colonial embroidery conventions.

Cloths were painted by hand in India, China, and Persia, some of them reaching the colonies, usually via Europe. Printed cloths, imitations of painted fabrics, were made in England and France from wood blocks and copperplate engravings, the latter being used for printing on silk, and for transferring the more complex designs to linen and cotton. These colorful materials became so popular that in 1700 Parliament sought to encourage domestic industry by prohibiting the importation of painted cloths, and in 1722 went further and prohibited the use of dyed, painted, or printed calicoes for apparel or furniture coverings.

There are no well-documented lines of direct connection between patterned fabrics and embroidery designs, but imported textiles were certainly one of the influential media by which design evolution in Europe was graphically portrayed to the colonists. That colonial women found them enticing is amply documented by the variety of wares "just Imported from London, all of the Newest Fashion," offered by drapers, stationers, and other shopkeepers who stocked fabrics and other items.

Wallpaper.

An invention of the late sixteenth century, wallpaper, came into general use in Europe late in the seventeenth century. Its contemporary name, "paper hangings," points to its original purpose: to provide a relatively inexpensive substitute for the costly decorative hangings of the wealthy. As may be surmised, wallpaper designs were closely associated with those of figured textiles.

The first decorative fabrics to be copied on paper were tapestries, followed by other figured woven stuffs, chiefly damasks, brocades, and velvets. Papers made after the manner of painted and printed fabrics are especially interesting, for they were most closely related to contemporary embroidery designs. In them, the fashion for floral and geometric patterns had a delightfully free expression and a flowing rhythm which could not be duplicated in woven materials.

While paper hangings could not match the warmth of the best of these exquisite painted and printed fabrics, the designs themselves were often just as charmingly conceived and as skillfully executed on paper as on fabric.

Existing examples of some lovely old colonial papers are so close to the embroidery idiom that a question naturally arises: Did papermakers lend inspiration to embroiderers, or was it the other way around? Probably a little of both; it seems inappropriate to assume the flow was wholly in either direction.

The period during which paper hangings were inspired by textile designs ran from the late seventeenth century to the late eighteenth century, with these imitative papers losing favor just before the Early American period was lost in fashion's genuflections toward Victorianism.

Wallpaper was first offered in colonial newspapers during the 1730's, but these announcements were not very informative as to patterns available. A half-century later advertisements were more numerous, stocks carried by colonial shops greatly enlarged, and prices correspondingly cheaper. One shopkeeper advertised that papering was less expensive than whitewashing! It is from the latter half of the eighteenth century that most of our existing wallpaper examples have been preserved.

Practically all figured fabrics and papers were imported and incorporated designs popular in Europe at the time. From them and other sources, colonial needlewomen took design ideas, adapted them to their own tastes, and in so doing helped create an embroidery tradition which has endured to this day.

Imported Embroideries.

It is hard to determine the extent of finished imported embroideries available to the colonists; records are sparse and scattered in about as many places as there were ports of entry.

Newspaper advertisements were full of references to imports of figured and flowered fabrics, but nothing about "work'd" or "wrought" materials. This strongly suggests that embroidered pieces were not ordinary items of commerce. The most likely imports would be pieces specially commissioned by individuals to fill specific needs. Also, visitors or travelers returning to the colonies might bring with them embroideries acquired abroad.

The one category that appears well documented is costume decoration. Several excellent collections are housed at museums in this country. Much of this embroidery, especially on men's coats and waistcoats, was of French design. Some of the execution was also French, but the embroidery on a number of men's waistcoats was done in China. These designs and the execution (nearly always in silk) were most attractive, and the workmanship exquisite. Isolated motifs from these elegant pieces may have been occasionally selected for adaptation to other uses but, in general, embroidery used on men's apparel was not readily translated to other applications.

There was considerably more flexibility in using embroideries adorning women's clothing. The border design on a dress might, with equal felicity, be adapted to other borders, to that of a coverlet, for instance. Wherever designs could be attractively adapted, they were freely interchanged.

Embroidery was one of colonial women's most splendid accomplishments. In most cases it was done within the home. There was seldom a need to have embroideries worked abroad except under the most unusual circumstances requiring custom design and execution by specialists in England or on the Continent.

Portraitists and Itinerant Artists.

One of the interesting facets of early American designs is the number of surviving embroideries that show evidence of skilled guidance in achieving balance, repose, and graceful disposition of lines. The "primitives" that have come down to the present day are largely those whose naïve charms partially, if not fully, compensate for their artistic deficiencies.

How could colonial needlewomen in the midst of their often meager resources, and the enormous demands upon their basic energies, have created so much that was good? Primarily, perhaps, because colonial women were required to depend upon their own resources for the creation of so many household necessities they could not permit any talents, latent or active, to lie dormant. In more affluent societies, women could declare an inability to do this or that for no other reason than a disinclination to try. Colonial women had to try, and in so doing, called into being a panorama of creativity rarely attained in a more leisured environment.

A contemporary evaluation of women's artistic capabilities is given by Archibald Robertson, an artist and teacher, in his *Elements of the Graphic Arts* (1802). He comments on America's prominent artists and continues:

> . . . many names could be added to those mentioned, who do honor to American genius, both professional, and of those who cultivate the graphic arts for instruction and pleasure; particularly ladies, whose performances are not only the admiration of the present day, but will very probably be held up as models at a future period.

Professional assistance in varying degrees of competence was often available, especially in urban areas along the seaboard, where the talents of teachers and artisans skilled in the decorative arts could be engaged. Peter Pelham, stepfather of John Singleton Copley, found it necessary to supplement his income from painting by offering instruction in various subjects:

Famed American painter Gilbert Stuart portrayed two elegant young cousins, Miss Dick and Miss Forster, in the process of preparing a design for embroidery.

Courtesy Mr. and Mrs. R. Philip Hane, Jr.

TERMS AND CONDITIONS
OF THE
BOARDING SCHOOL
FOR
FEMALE EDUCATION
IN
SALEM, N. C.

THE age of admittance of pupils is between 8 and 12 years. The age of 15 terminates their stay in the School: unless parents choose, to order their return home sooner, or their deportment should be such, as not to admit their continuance in the School.

Every attention is paid to the health and morals of the pupils.

The branches taught are: Reading, Grammar, Writing, Arithmetic, History, Geography, plain Needlework, &c. Music and fine Needlework, including Drawing are two extra branches, in which instruction is given, if expressly desired.

Entrance money is 5 Dollars.

The quarterly expence for board and tuition, bedding included, is at present 24 Dollars, to be advanced every quarter. Washing is ~~a separate charge, viz.~~ *included.* ~~Dollars per quarter for pupils under 12 years, and Dollars for those above that age.~~ For instruction in Music and fine Needlework, each 2 Dollars per quarter. Cloathing, medecine, books, paper and other contingent expences are charged quarterly.

Punctual payment of the bills is expected, and a settlement in full at the removal of children.

The amount of the yearly expences collectively may be calculated at the rate of between 160 and 180 Dollars, more or less.

Parents may either, if they have it convenient, furnish the articles of cloathing, or the pupils may be found here.

Every article of cloathing, they bring along, should be marked, so as to stand washing.

The dress to be decent, avoiding extravagance.

Aplications are to be made in writing, addressed to the Rev. Abraham Steiner, the present inspector of the Seminary at Salem, N. C.; informing him of the age, name and character of the child, the name and place of residence of the parents, guardians, &c. and it is requested, that no child may be brought or sent without leave obtained from him in writing, appointing the time of admittance. It is desirable, that such as are applied for, should have had the small or kine pox and measles.

Parents and guardians &c. may rest assured, that the undersigned will endeavour to merit their confidence, by paying the most faithful attention to the education of the pupils intrusted to his care.

Salem, N. C.

18. December 1815.

Abraham Steiner

"Plain Needlework" and "fine Needlework" were among the subjects taught in 1815 at a "Boarding School for Female Education" in Salem, North Carolina.

Courtesy Tennessee State Library and Archives

Possibly used for instructional purposes, this late seventeenth-century English sampler shows popular floral motifs.

Courtesy The Connecticut Historical Society

Flowers, ruins, and various devices, along with the familiar alphabet and numerals, were featured in this silk embroidery worked by Catharina Kieslich in 1809. It may have been a teaching sampler.

Courtesy Museum of the City of New York

Mr. Peter Pelham gives notice to all Gentlemen and Ladies in Town and Country, That at the House of Philip Dumerisque, Esq. in Summer street (next his own Dwelling house) Young Gentlemen and Ladies may be Taught Dancing, Writing, Reading, painting upon Glass, and all sorts of needle work.

Boston *Gazette,* February, 1738

In more remote communities, women were likely to call upon the diverse talents of occasional itinerant painters who traveled from town to town throughout the colonies, tarrying as long as their services were in demand.

Portrait painting was the most prestigious and sought-after engagement, but relatively few itinerant artists had sufficient competence in this field to rely upon "face painting," as it was sometimes called, as their mainstay. As a result, they eked out their sometimes precarious livelihoods by turning to an amazing variety of collateral activities associated with the decorative arts. Newspaper advertisements show them offering all manner of services: portraits, miniatures, hair work "in the most elegant manner," limning, altarpieces, landscapes, signs, historical pieces, perspective views of gentlemen's country seats, painting on silk or satin, coach and chaise painting in all its branches, with arms, ciphers, ornamentals of every kind, pictures copied, cleansed, or mended, fans painted, family and conversation pieces, crests, heraldry, prints colored, painting inside of houses to represent stucco, fret, or carved work, screens, gilding, pictures framed, paper hanging, engravings, all kinds of drawing, picture panels over chimney-pieces, and so on.

Competence in portrait painting ran the gamut from unschooled mediocrity to commercial acceptability. Nearly all itinerant artists who undertook portraits, however deficient they might be in the nuances of portraiture, were skilled in reproducing the laces, embroidery, and jewelry adorning their subjects. Of this there is ample evidence in early portraits. Apparently their sitters were often as much, or more, concerned that their sartorial elegancies be faithfully recorded as they were that their persons be reproduced with fidelity. In fact a little flattery of face or figure might not be at all displeasing.

It seems reasonable to conclude that such skills as these itinerants possessed in meticulously depicting needlework designs in apparel worn by their subjects were often put to service in assisting colonial women to lay out their own designs. In this the itinerant artisans were undoubtedly quite competent; flat surface work was, after all, much less demanding than a rendering of the contours and configurations of their sitters.

Compiling an all-inclusive register of information about early American embroideries is virtually impossible. The subject is too complex, the time span too great, to be within the purview of any one person. Therein lies both an invitation and a challenge to all who enjoy explorations into the rich heritages our forebears wrought in the decorative arts.

The flavor of a bygone age cannot be recaptured in ink on paper. At best we can only illuminate fragments here and there, and perhaps, like "fire-flies innumerous spangling o'er the vale," add a little to the pleasure of those who tarry for a moment of quiet appreciation.

Notices

Mrs. Phinney would like to instruct a few young Ladies in Drawing, Painting, Gilding, and Embroidery. Reading, English Grammar and Geography will be attended if desired.
American Recorder, Washington, D.C., July, 1819

Peter Hall, Upholsterer, in Chestnut-street, makes all Sorts of Beds, Chairs, or any other Furniture fir for any house: Also will teach any Person to draw Draughts in a short time for Flourishing or Embroidering, at the most reasonable rates.
Pennsylvania *Gazette,* April, 1745

John Anthony Beau . . . being lately arrived in this city from Geneva, Takes this method to recommend himself to the favour of the Public, and acquaints them that he performes all sorts of chasing work in gold, silver, and other metals . . . in the genteelest and newest taste. He likewise offers his services to teach Ladies Drawing, and to give them the best principles to learn very soon, let it be figures, ornaments, flowers, or designs for embroidering, &c.
Pennsylvania *Packet,* July, 1772

As I purpose to teach Drawing and Embroidery, this is to give Notice, that I shall open School the first of May next, at Miss Elizabeth Murphy's in King-street, where good Attendance shall be given, and the Scholars carefully instructed. I will also take in Drawing and plain Work, Washing and Ironing Ladies Head-Cloaths, in the best Manner and at a reasonable Rate, and shall be much obliged to any Lady that will favour me with their Custom. Magdalene Hamilton.
South Carolina *Gazette,* April, 1748

Mr. Buriat, Just arrived from Cape Francaise, Has the honor to inform the public, that he embroiders on and with all kinds of materials, such as gold, silver, silk, cotton, wll, thread, on all sorts of woollen, silk, lawn, cambric, linen, cotton, &c. He embroiders coats of arms in the most delicate stile. . . . He lives in New-street, No. 65, between Second and Third streets.
Federal Gazette, Philadelphia, June, 1794

An assortment of colonial newspaper advertisements about embroidery and other allied arts.

CHAPTER ONE

BED FURNISHINGS

By far the largest number of colonial embroideries which have survived (samplers excepted) are bed furnishings of one kind or another. Many which have withstood the ravages of time are preserved in museums, restored historic houses, and in private collections. Unfortunately, only a few complete sets remain in existence, such as those in the Old Gaol Museum in York, Maine. A few motifs from this set are shown in Plate 7.

A well-dressed bed was an object of great pride, and more often than not was the *pièce de résistance* of the main room of the house. The colonial embroiderer's finest skills went into making furnishings for it, since such items were invariably the most prominent in her household, and she would want them to display her workmanship at its very best.

Bed furnishings usually consisted of these elements:

Curtains, also called hangings, were usually made of four pieces: two wide panels for the foot and two narrower panels for the head. All four pieces could be pulled around the sides of the bed for about half its length so that the bed could be fully enclosed.

Valances, also called vallens, were made in three or four pieces, each usually ten to twelve inches wide. If the bed was placed against the wall, only three were needed. If it stood away from the wall, four were required. Few four-poster beds were without them. These might be embroidered, with the remainder of the bed furnishings perfectly plain. If not embroidered, they would usually be made of figured fabrics appropriate to a well-dressed bed. They were usually shaped slightly along the lower edge and were designed to be hung flat and fairly taut along a tester frame. Often the contours of the design itself determined the shape of the valance; a valance in which the design incorporated undulating vines might well have shallow scallops along its lower edge. These pieces were commonly attached to a bed frame in various ways, usually by means of eyelet holes which fitted onto hooks secured to the frame, or by a cord strung through a casing along the top edge of the valance, the cord being attached to the bedposts at the four corners.

Bases, also referred to as flounces, were "valances" for the lower part of the bed frame. Today they are more likely to be called "dust ruffles." They were made to hang as a cover for the space between the bed frame and the floor.

A counterpane, also known as a coverlet, coverlid, or bed cover, covered the entire top surface of the bed. This piece was sometimes made with sides long enough to hang to the floor, thus eliminating the need for separate bases.

A head cloth, also called a tester, was a wide panel hung at the head of the bed, and was the focal point of the bed furnishings. Its design was nearly always related to the one on the coverlet. These head cloths were usually hung flat, not gathered, normally falling below the bottom of the headboard.

The shapes and sizes of bed furnishings varied, of course, as did the designs worked upon them. Some motifs were quite ornate, some light and airy, some fanciful, and some almost stark in their simplicity. The edges of coverlets, valances, and curtains could be trimmed in various ways: with hand-tied or ball fringes, tassels, or tapes sewn along the edges as a finish.

Yarn and thread preferred for embroidering varied with climatic conditions along the eastern seaboard. Little crewelwork has been documented as originating in the warmer, more humid regions, but crewels were popular along the northern coastal plain. Certain color combinations were popular throughout the colonies. White-on-white was universally popular (as it had been in Europe for generations). Two other favored combinations were blue and rose and blue and white. Remarkable examples of southern needlewomen's use of these combinations may be seen in the color section.

Pages 38-41.
Flowers and fruit worked in crewels provide motifs for a New England bed valance of 1714.

Courtesy Museum of Fine Arts, Boston, Helen and Alice Colburn Fund

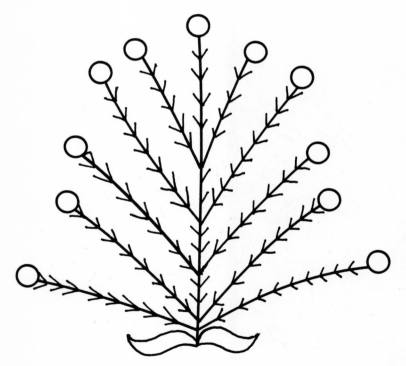

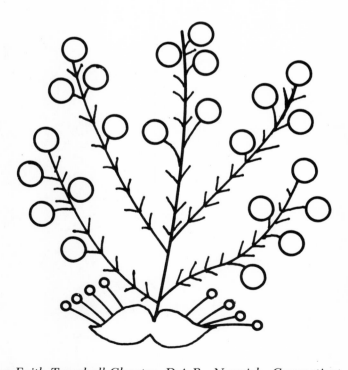

Pages 45 - 47.
Bed hangings embroidered by Eunice Brewster about 1765 include a variety of floral motifs.

Courtesy Faith Trumbull Chapter, D.A.R., Norwich, Connecticut

Pages 48 - 51.
This bed cover is embroidered in crewels with figures of a man and woman dressed in contemporary costumes under a tree filled with birds. The inscription reads "E. S. Brewster, Roxbury." It is believed to have been made by Elizabeth Swan Brewster (1741 - 1817), who married Daniel Brewster in 1764.

Courtesy The Connecticut Historical Society

Bed furnishings occupied a prominent place in colonial interiors. This scrolled bed cover was the property of the John Hancock family of Massachusetts. It is shown in Plate 1.

Courtesy Henry Francis du Pont Winterthur Museum

Also from Massachusetts, though presumed older than the bed cover, is a head cloth which incorporates a scrolled woolen and silk tape appliquéd to the background, with embroidery worked over and around in a trellis effect. It is interesting to note the striking similarity between the two designs.

Courtesy of the author

These eighteenth-century valances, once part of a set of bed hangings, have motifs of birds and flowers worked in crewels in shades of blue. (See Plate 3 for a view of these valances.)

Courtesy Essex Institute, Salem, Massachusetts

FLORAL DESIGNS

The most popular designs for household embroideries were those created around floral motifs. Women everywhere enjoyed the bounty and color of nature, a pleasure the English long reflected in their love of gardens. There was much correspondence between the colonies and England about flora unique to America and the successes or failures attending efforts to introduce our plants and flowers to England, and vice versa.

Where better could an embroiderer seek inspiration intermingling fascinating colors, lovely forms, and graceful lines than in nature itself? Roses, carnations, tulips, berries, leaves, fruits, small plants, vines, and tendrils were the predominant elements of floral designs, often accompanied by a random bird, a butterfly or two, an insect, or a familiar animal gracing the background. Occasionally an ornamental device, perhaps a basket, would be included.

Floral designs, particularly the more elaborate ones, demanded polychrome treatment, if not the full spectrum of nature, then as close to it as the embroiderer's resources permitted. Fortunate were those who had, or could obtain, threads to work a full polychrome color scheme.

Monochromatic color planning was also used. This choice may, of course, have been determined by the availability of materials; even the most skilled embroiderer could work only with what was at hand or readily obtained. Perhaps some needlewomen, insecure in their color skills, preferred monochrome rather than accept the challenge of a more demanding and elaborate color scheme. Others preferred blue-on-white above all, and would have nothing else; the "blue tub," or indigo pot, in the kitchen was certainly in frequent use. Whatever the reasons, many lovely designs in monochrome have been preserved.

It is necessary to examine many of these pieces in detail to appreciate fully the remarkable needle artistry of colonial women. It is not unusual to find an entire piece done with three or four simple stitches. On the other hand, many embroiderers displayed a large and impressive repertoire. Among favorite stitches were straight, chain, outline, Roumanian, French knots, buttonhole, satin, herringbone, cross, fishbone, seed, and feather.

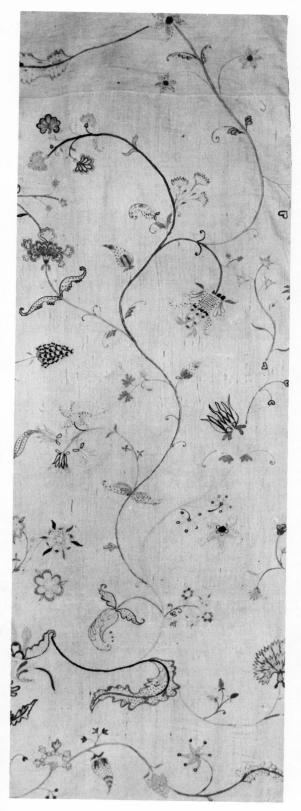

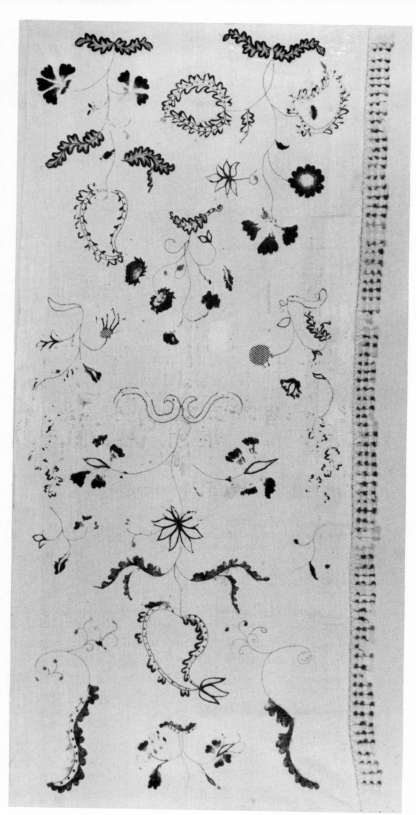

Floral motifs were consistently popular for curtains, valances, and borders, as shown here in the panel and curtain with ball-fringed edge, believed to have been made about 1800.

These floral borders bear initials, probably those of the embroiderer's.

Courtesy The Cooper-Hewitt Museum of Design

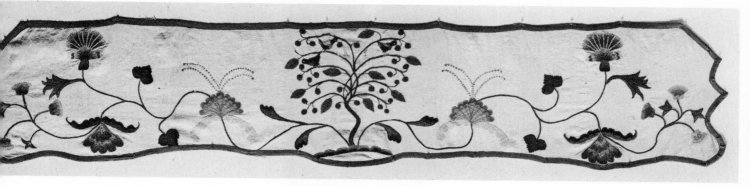

A solid border encloses the design for this eighteenth-century valance. (For a view of this piece in color, see Plate 5.)

Courtesy Museum of Fine Arts, Boston, Helen and Alice Colburn Fund

Sarah Brewster worked this floral motif in 1776.

Courtesy Museum of Fine Arts, Boston, Gift of Mrs. Althea Carr Roach and Mrs. Samuel Cabot

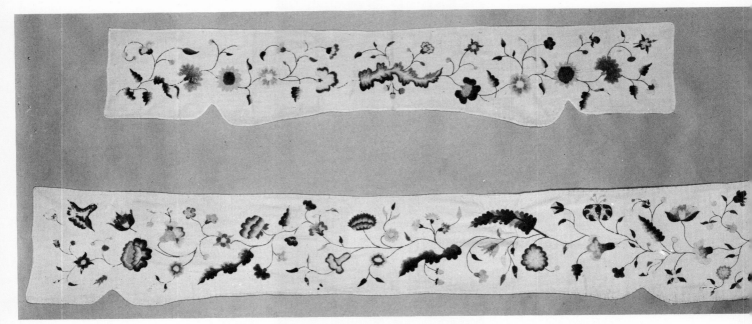

Two mid-eighteenth-century valances from Kensington, New Hampshire, were embroidered on a linen and cotton ground.

Courtesy Museum of Fine Arts, Boston, Harriet Otis Cruft Fund; Special Textile Fund

opposite
Crewels highlighted by polychrome silks were used to work motifs in the Low estate bed cover, made about 1750. (For views of motifs of this cover, see Plate 4.)

Courtesy Brooklyn Museum

Fanciful birds and beasts abound in this eighteenth-century embroidered quilt.

Courtesy Brooklyn Museum

This eighteenth-century cover with richly worked borders and scattered center motifs was embroidered on linen in bright crewels.

Courtesy The Metropolitan Museum of Art, Gift of Mr. and Mrs. Frank Coit Johnson, 1944

Worked by Lucinda Coleman, this eighteenth-century cover has many floral designs.
(For motifs from the cover, see Plate 6.)

Courtesy The Metropolitan Museum of Art, Sansbury-Mills Fund, 1961

Plate 1.

Embroidered with linen and wool, a bed cover of tabby-woven linen dated 1749 (*top left*) is an early example of American needlework. The initials "CBR" and "PTB" are believed to stand for Catherine and Peter Ten Broeck. Floral sprays are embroidered on a light blue background in an eighteenth-century New England bed cover (*top right*). Contemporary printed textiles such as this copperplate-printed tabby-weave cotton from England (*center left*) were among the popular sources for embroidery motifs. Covering a four-poster bed from a Newport home, the scrolled bed cover with hanging bases (*bottom right*) was owned by the John Hancock family of Massachusetts.

Top left: *Courtesy Colonial Williamsburg*

Top right: *Courtesy Essex Institute, Salem, Massachusetts*

Center left: *Courtesy Colonial Williamsburg*

Bottom right: *Courtesy Henry Francis du Pont Winterthur Museum*

65

Plate 2.

Floral designs embroidered on linen in polychrome crewels are characteristic of mid-eighteenth-century bed furnishings.

Courtesy Colonial Williamsburg

66

Plate 3.

A monochromatic color scheme was popular with eighteenth-century American embroiderers. Shades of blue crewels were highly effective against light-colored backgrounds of home-spun fabrics.

Courtesy Essex Institute, Salem, Massachusetts

Courtesy Brooklyn Museum

Plates 4 and 5.

Birds, flowers, and fruit were motifs used by colonial needlewomen, who often adapted designs from animals and plants observed in their gardens and neighboring woodlands.

Courtesy Faith Trumbull Chapter, D.A.R., Norwich, Connecticut

Courtesy Brooklyn Museum

69

Plate 6.

Blossoms, seedpods, acorns, and foliage provided further design motifs for colonial needlewomen.

Courtesy The Metropolitan Museum of Art, Purchase, 1961, Sansbury-Mills Fund

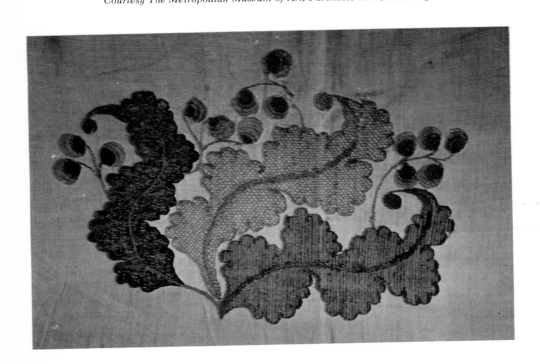

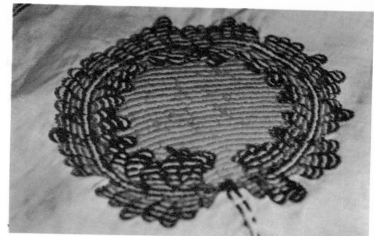

Plate 7.

Surface stitches, an economy measure frequently practiced in colonial America to conserve yarn, were often used for floral and arboreal motifs in curtains and canopies. The motif (*top,* showing both right side and wrong side) was taken from a bed cover made by Lucy Bliss of Massachusetts. The set of bed hangings in which the motifs (*center right* and *bottom*) are included was made in 1745 by Mrs. Mary Bulman of York, Maine.

Top: *Courtesy Heritage Foundation, Deerfield, Massachusetts*

Center right and bottom: *Courtesy Old Gaol Museum, York, Maine*

Plate 8.

Embroidery provides additional detail on the appliquéd cover of designs cut from English chintz with the squares joined by strips of calico. It was made about 1770 by ladies of the Berkeley and Westover plantations in Virginia.

Courtesy The Valentine Museum, Richmond, Virginia

Plate 9.

Exotic birds and an elaborate floral border placed in a central medallion are features of this appliquéd bed cover (*top*). Motifs cut from India prints were appliquéd on an eighteenth-century "story coverlet" (*bottom*).

Top: *Courtesy Museum of Early Southern Decorative Arts, Old Salem, North Carolina*

Bottom: *Courtesy Brooklyn Museum*

Plate 10.

Rose and blue cotton embroidered in a bowknot motif is one of the design ideas used in a Pennsylvania-German cover (*top*), probably made about 1800. The red handwoven tablecloth (*bottom*), embroidered in white with a basket of flowers motif, dates from the eighteenth century.

Top: *Courtesy of the author*

Bottom: *Courtesy The Denver Art Museum*

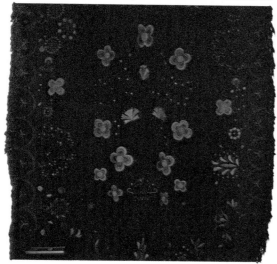

Plate 11.

Embroidered with polychrome crewels on black woolen twill, the coverlet (*top left*) was made in 1760 by Harriet (or Hannah) Dunbar of Lenox, Massachusetts. She also wove and dyed the wool. The eighteenth-century woolen coverlet embroidered in wool (*top right*) is from the Connecticut Valley. The coverlet with the blue wool background (*bottom left*) is a fine example of eighteenth-century work. Another eighteenth-century coverlet (*bottom right*) was embroidered by Mary Stover with polychrome crewels on blue-green wool twill and has hand-tied tassels.

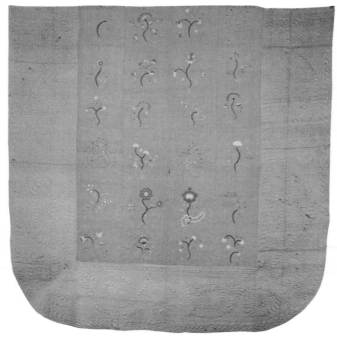

Plate 12.

Silk is used for embroidery and button coverings on a pale gray wool waistcoat (*top left*) of about 1780 worn by General Lewis Littlepage of Hanover County, Virginia. A design embroidered in crewels borders the muslin dress (*bottom left*) dating from the early nineteenth century, as does the child's dress (*bottom center*), embroidered in pink and green crewels. The child's dress (*bottom right*) has a green and white color scheme worked in linen threads.

Courtesy The Valentine Museum, Richmond, Virginia

Courtesy The Denver Art Museum

Courtesy Essex Institute, Salem, Massachusetts

Courtesy Heritage Foundation, Deerfield, Massachusetts

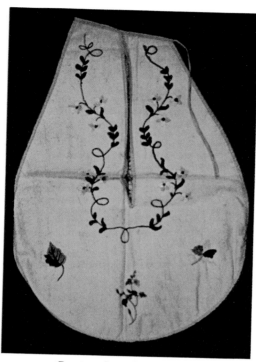

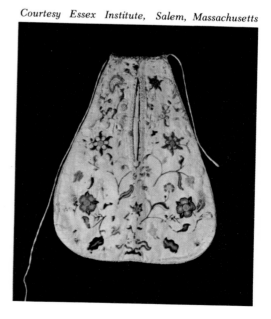

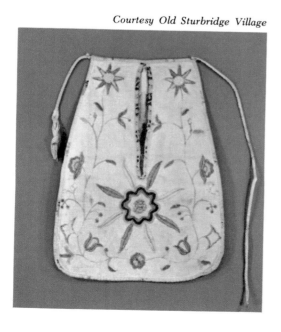

Plate 13.

Polychrome crewels are embroidered on a petticoat border (*top right*) and three linen pockets (*top left* and *bottom*).

Plate 14.

Wool, silk, and metal threads were used in a needlework picture made in mid-eighteenth-century New England (*top*). A chair seat (*center*) and picture (*bottom*) are both canvas work, the chair seat featuring the popular carnation motif. Sarah Chamberlain embroidered the picture about 1764.

Top: *Courtesy Museum of Fine Arts, Boston, Gift of Mrs. Samuel Cabot*

Center: *Courtesy Museum of Fine Arts, Boston, Gift of Mrs. Kennard Winsor*

Bottom: *Courtesy Essex Institute, Salem, Massachusetts*

Plate 15.

Embroidered in silk about 1750 by the wife of Governor Gabriel Johnson of North Carolina, the picture subject (*top*) has a painted face and arms. Another example of silk embroidery from North Carolina, the picture (*center*) dates from the late eighteenth century. An old church at Stone Ridge, New York, is shown in a silk embroidery picture (*bottom*). It was done by Rachel Broadhead as a schoolgirl in 1812.

Top and center: *Courtesy State Department of Archives and History, Raleigh, North Carolina*

Bottom: *Courtesy Minneapolis Institute of Arts*

Plate 16.

Three early American samplers show needlework exercises expected of properly trained young ladies. The sampler (*top left*) was made in New England in 1794. Rebekah Ursula Ousby of Raleigh, North Carolina, worked the sampler (*top right*) about 1834. The sampler (*bottom*) was made by Lucinda Ishs, Loudoun County, Virginia, in 1812.

Embroidered on linen in bright crewels, this valance has finely wrought motifs and borders.

Courtesy The Art Institute of Chicago

Only portions remain of the two borders for valances made about 1790 by Hannah Larabee Willis, married in 1789 to Asa Willis in Bennington, Vermont.

83

A vase of flowers forms the central motif in this eighteenth-century New England bed cover.

Courtesy Museum of Fine Arts, Boston, Gift of Miss G. Emery

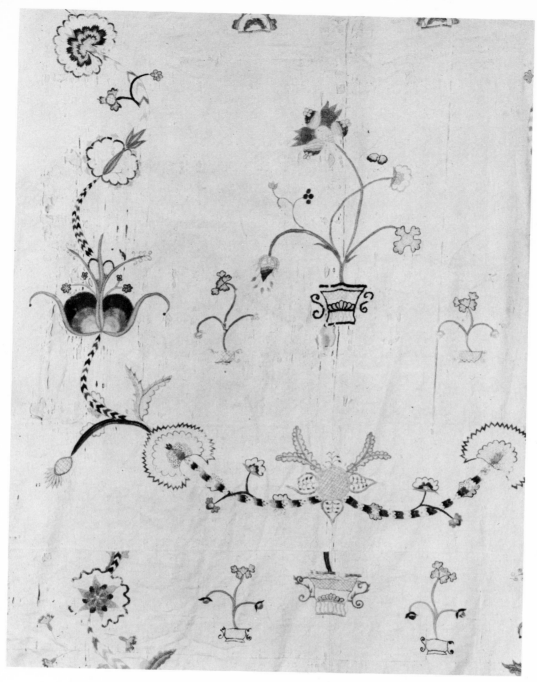

Flowers are the central motif of this bed cover.

Courtesy Brooklyn Museum

opposite, bottom

A ship, seldom used in early American embroidery designs, is featured in this embroidered cotton panel. It dates from the early eighteenth century.

Courtesy The Art Institute of Chicago

Crewels in values of blue have been used on the eighteenth-century linen bed cover *(left)* from the Low estate. (For a motif from this cover, see Plate 4.) In the eighteenth-century cover from Connecticut *(right)* the design has been worked in blue crewels on cream wool. The cotton bed cover *(below),* dating from the second half of the eighteenth century, has been embroidered in blue wool.

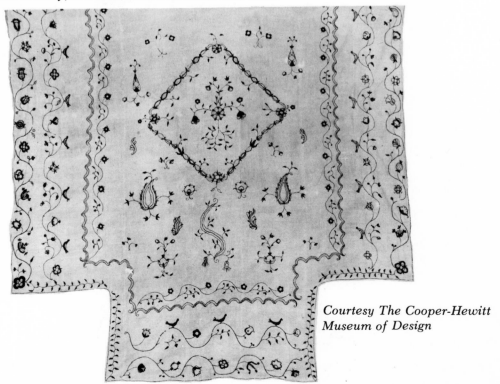

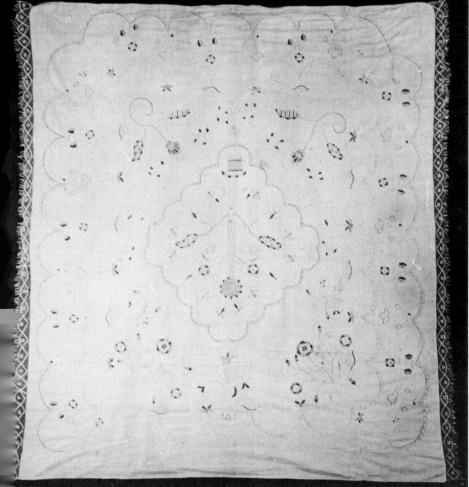

above

The coverlet, inscribed "Jane. Cooper. November 28. 1823," made in South Carolina, is embroidered in values of blue and rose cotton on a hand-woven cotton homespun.

Courtesy Mrs. Chisholm Wallace

Also embroidered in blue and rose cotton is a coverlet inscribed "B A/ 1807," the initials standing for Elizabeth "Bess" Abrams of Newberry County, South Carolina.

Courtesy Museum of Early Southern Decorative Arts, Old Salem, North Carolina

87

A German inscription including the name "Katerina," the word "geborren" (born), and faded dates including "Ano 1787" is embroidered on this table cover in which decorative motifs are used with great restraint.

Courtesy Henry Francis du Pont Winterthur Museum

This Pennsylvania-German coverlet, embroidered in blue and rose cotton on white cotton twill with a "satin" finish, was probably made in the early 1800's. (For a view of a motif in color, see Plate 10.)

Courtesy of the author

QUILTS: PLAIN, PATCHWORK, AND EMBROIDERED

Patience and superb needle skills are evident in the various examples of early American quilts, some embroidered, some appliquéd, some combinations of both techniques. Quilting itself was an old art when the first settlers brought it to this country. Techniques for making quilts by hand remain about the same to this day.

For plain quilts, the quilting pattern was drawn onto the upper layer of the quilt before it was placed in the quilting frame with the underlayer. Usually there was some padding between the two layers, the padding being increased as needed to accentuate the "puffed" effect. Then the quilting design would be worked through the entire thickness of the assembled materials with fine running stitches, thus creating a quilted effect. For an embroidered quilt the embroidery would first be completed on the top layer, then this piece, with the underlayer and padding, would be assembled in the frame, and the quilting pattern stitched over the entire surface. This produced an interesting effect upon the embroidery by suggesting another dimension.

Salvaging pieces of cloth by sewing them together to make something usable was especially necessary in the colonial period. Patchwork quilt designs were conceived and worked to make "new" bed coverings from garments and other household fabrics no longer usable. The finished piece was all the more cherished for being made of bits and pieces of materials associated with happy memories of the past. After the top layer of the quilt had been assembled by patchwork, the procedures followed those used in making plain quilts, even to embroidering the top layer if desired before the final quilting assembly. Occasionally, the top layer would be assembled from pieces of embroidered materials cut into shape to fit the patchwork pattern, often resulting in highly imaginative designs.

The animal designs worked for a patchwork quilt now in the collection of Old Sturbridge Village form a menagerie of amazing variety. One can only assume its embroiderer was widely traveled or widely read, with the added advantage of an unfettered imagination. Unfortunately, this quilt was never completed; only the upper piece was worked on.

Animals were favorite subjects for many embroideries — birds on the wing or nestled on a branch or vine, insects of all kinds flitting hither and yon. Dogs, squirrels, rabbits, deer, and many other familiar animals, as much part of the local scene as the woods and flowers, were often pictured beneath a tree or upon a small hillock.

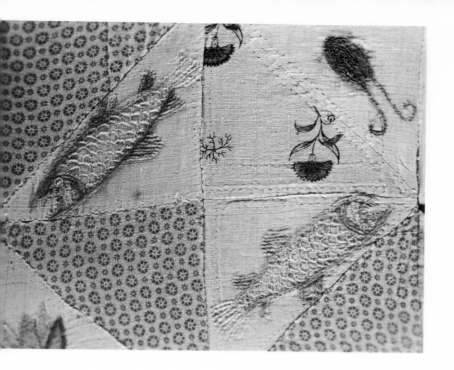

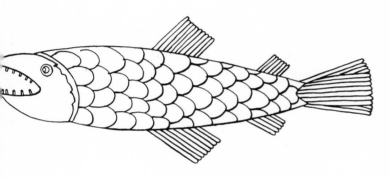

Pages 90 - 93.
The animal kingdom is well represented in an embroidered quilt made in Haverhill, Massachusetts, about 1750. A vase of flowers and a pair of fish are included in the design, along with a miscellany of real and imaginary birds and beasts.

Courtesy Old Sturbridge Village

APPLIQUÉ

The fine art of applying one material onto the base of another is a form of decorative needlework which has been practiced for centuries. Designs are cut from one piece of material and secured with stitches to the background of another. The appliqued pieces may be printed motifs cut from patterned fabrics — or shapes from other materials cut according to the embroiderer's own fancy — flowers, small animals, geometric designs, leaves, and so on.

The availability of beautiful printed materials from abroad undoubtedly challenged the ingenuity of colonial needlewomen to appliqué some of these motifs onto base materials and thereby create a design with an added dimension of depth. Several interesting examples of appliqué are shown here. The bed cover from the Valentine Museum is a masterpiece in remarkable condition, one of the most delightfully conceived examples of its kind. The coverlet from the Museum of Early Southern Decorative Arts is an outstanding example of the skill required for the appliqué technique. The motifs, possibly inspired by the abounding wildlife of lower South Carolina, were painstakingly cut from an old piece of chintz and applied to the background with exquisitely fine stitches. The result is a tribute to the patience and finesse of colonial women determined to surround themselves with beauty whenever possible. In the charming coverlet from the Brooklyn Museum, a series of events, including a voyage and a presentation at court, is laid out in an appealing sequence and worked with an expertise that is a challenge to today's needlewomen.

This garland is a detail from an appliquéd bed cover made in South Carolina about 1800. (For views of this cover in color, see Plate 9.)

Courtesy Museum of Early Southern Decorative Arts, Old Salem, North Carolina

Pages 96 - 98.
Shown here are details from the West-over bed cover, an example of patch-work, appliqué, and embroidery, worked by the Byrd and Harrison ladies of the great Virginia plantations of Berkeley and Westover when they gathered every fortnight under a "trysting tree." The designs were cut from English chintz and appliquéd with colored silks onto fine unbleached cotton. Each set of the four corners, forming a square, was sewn together with strips of red and white calico. The general design includes a variety of embroidered details such as a squirrel on a mound, shaded petals, berries, and sprays of leaves. (For details in color, see Plate 8.)

Pages 99-101.
This unusual piece, including figures of soldiers on horseback and wagons, along with more familiar motifs of birds and flowers, is believed to depict events of the American Revolution.

Courtesy Brooklyn Museum

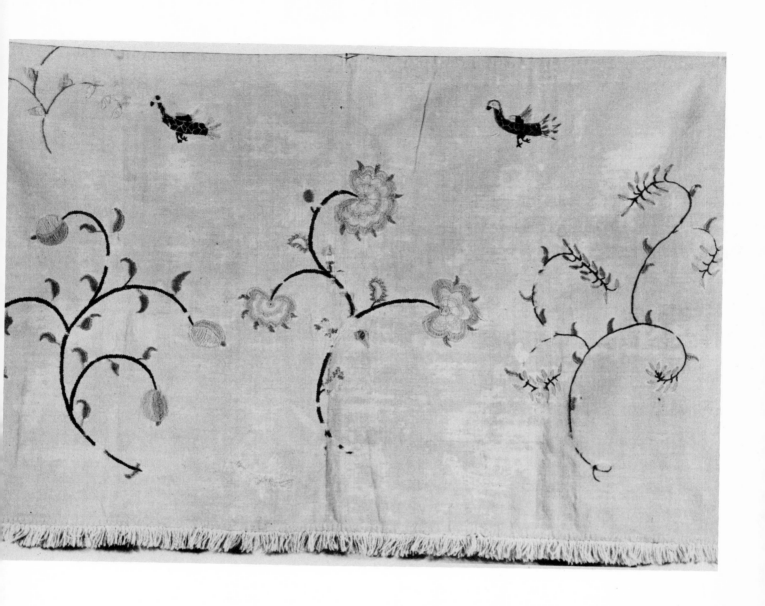

Pages 102 - 104.
This eighteenth-century "story coverlet" combines a rare collection of India prints from England appliquéd on a white hand-woven linen background with an overall quilted design. Such story coverlets were occasionally used to document events of public interest or highlights in the life of the maker, or her family. This coverlet apparently chronicles the life of a young married couple, including presentation at court and a voyage to a new home in a strange land. (See Plate 9.)

Courtesy Brooklyn Museum

104

The raised design of the white-on-white "Sally Grant coverlet" provides an interesting texture.

Courtesy Brooklyn Museum

WHITE WORK

White work is a broad term used to describe white embroidery on white backgrounds. This form of needlework covers a wide range of techniques, including Mountmellick, drawn thread and drawn fabric work, and so on. Examples of some particularly handsome pieces of early American white work are pictured here. Background materials varied from sheer to heavy, and were linen, cotton, or wool. The thread used also varied greatly in weight and type, from silk to wool. Dresses, bed covers, household and church linens were particularly adaptable to this technique. Stitches could be bold or varied, as in Mountmellick work, or very delicate if required by sheer materials. Texture variations by use of certain surface stitches were achieved with great charm and skill, in some cases the variation being nothing more than a change in the direction of the needle placement.

106

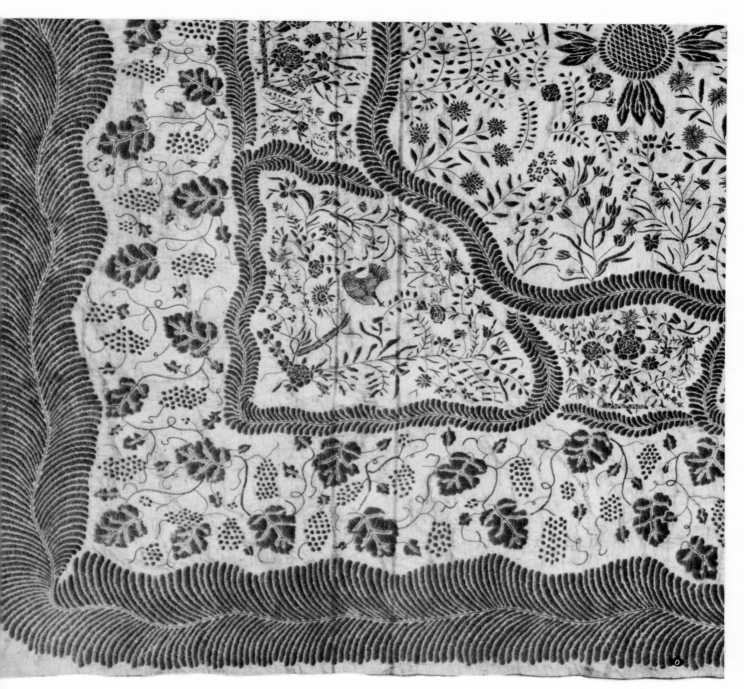

An all-white linen coverlet known as the "garden coverlet," made in 1810, is an example of detail and workmanship lavished on purely decorative bed coverings of the era. Included in the design are garden herbs, flowers and fruits, and even turkeys, worked in an "oriental" style. The center motif, or medallion, is a pomegranate, traditional symbol of growth and good fortune. The feather-design borders are done in "stuffed work," used also in defining other decorative elements of the coverlet.

Courtesy Brooklyn Museum

An example of early designs which continued into much later periods is this linen and cotton coverlet embroidered with white-on-white and incorporating some exquisite drawnwork in the motifs. It was worked in Kentucky about 1800 - 1810 by Amelia Chenoweth Nash, wife of Colonel Harmon Nash. Several motifs are shown here in detail.

Courtesy Museum of Early Southern Decorative Arts,
Old Salem, North Carolina

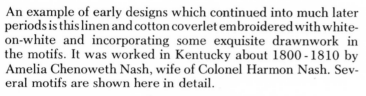

Made during the second half of the eighteenth century, this coverlet is embroidered in heavy white cotton thread on white cotton homespun. It was once the property of Anne Rector Conway, who was born in Virginia and went to Tennessee with Henry Conway, father of Thomas Conway, founder of the state.

Courtesy The Cooper-Hewitt Museum of Design

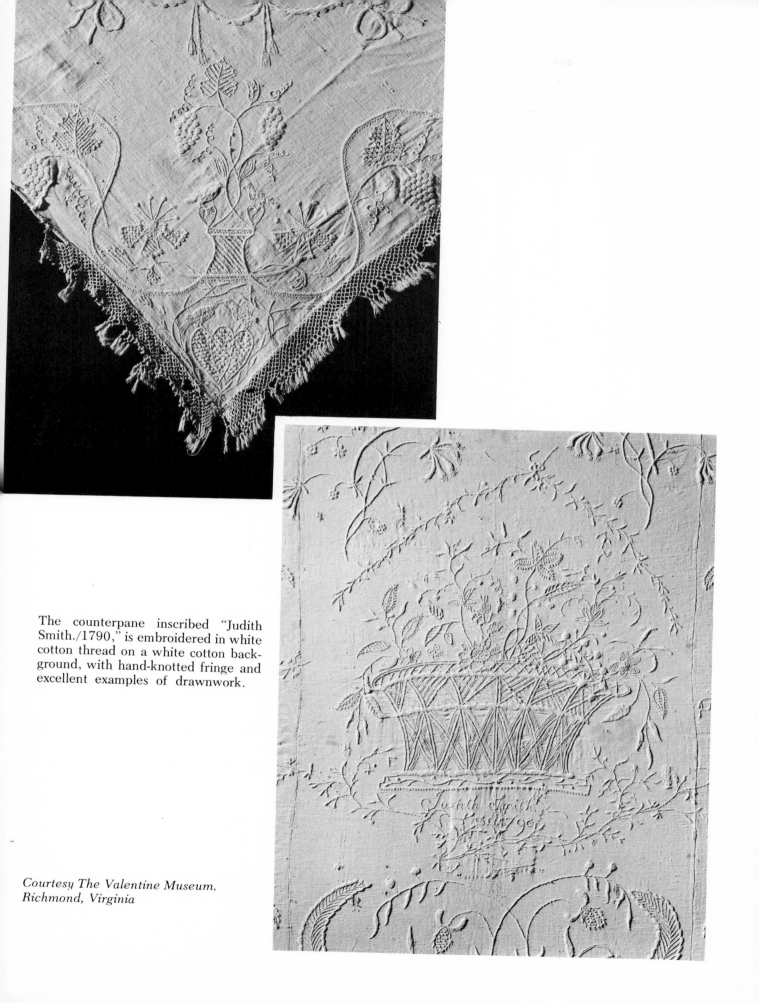

The counterpane inscribed "Judith Smith./1790," is embroidered in white cotton thread on a white cotton background, with hand-knotted fringe and excellent examples of drawnwork.

Courtesy The Valentine Museum, Richmond, Virginia

Made of two widths of cloth sewn together, the diaper-weave linen bed cover is embroidered in two shades of blue linen thread and has fringe on the sides and rounded corners.

Courtesy Henry Francis du Pont Winterthur Museum

BED RUGS

Noah Webster's first dictionary (1806) defined a rug as a "rough woollen coverlet for beds." When embroidered they were usually worked with woolen yarn, creating a heavy wool-on-wool texture. Typically, the surface was well covered with large, bold designs that left little background exposed, a treatment generally requiring stitches made with two or more strands of yarn. Embroidered bed rugs such as the colorful examples shown here provided warmth and added a decorative note. This type of bed cover was, of course, most popular in northern regions of America where rigorous winters held sway. An elaborately embroidered bed rug was the pride of the whole family, often handed down from generation to generation.

This wool-embroidered coverlet was made in Connecticut by Amy Williams about 1799.

Courtesy The Cleveland Museum of Art

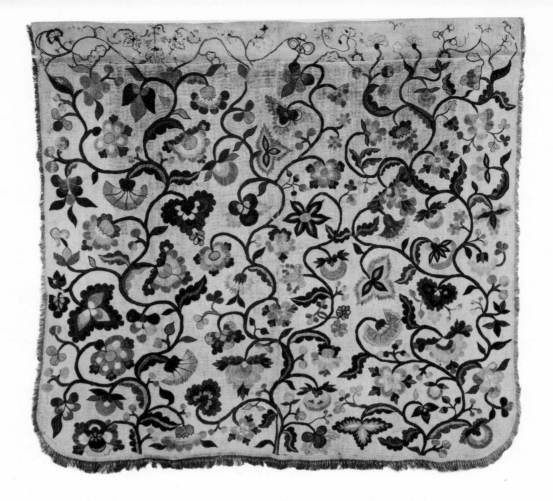

Handspun, woven, and dyed, this dark blue wool cover is embroidered in shades of tan and green wool and inscribed "Mercy Post.,/Newport.,/June 2nd 1824."

Courtesy The Art Institute of Chicago

opposite top

Crewel embroidery forms the pattern of this early eighteenth-century fringed bed rug. The background is linen and cotton woven in a twill diaper design; the lining is tabby-woven wool.

Courtesy Colonial Williamsburg

opposite below

Crewels in red, greens, and tan on a brown wool ground decorate a bed cover with green fringe, made about 1790.

Courtesy The Art Institute of Chicago

Animals, flowers, and pine trees, on a portion of a crewel-embroidered valance, are duplicated (in reduced scale) on the hem of the pocketed apron of an antique doll.

Courtesy Colonial Williamsburg

CHAPTER TWO

APPAREL AND ACCESSORIES

The colonial embroiderer expressed her skills and competence in needlework on many articles for the home, but her accomplishments indicate that much of her time was also spent on attractive clothing for her family. Numerous embroidered items, from nightcaps to wedding gowns, bear testimony to the needlework skills practiced by the never-idle hands of busy colonial needlewomen.

Designs of great charm, simplicity, and beauty, were carefully worked upon all manner of personal apparel: slippers, caps, border designs for skirts, petticoats, aprons, cuffs and collars, finely worked bands, even elaborately embroidered dresses and waistcoats. A miniature design worked upon a doll's tiny apron suggests a pleasure shared by both mother and daughter in dressing a favorite doll.

Petticoat borders served a dual purpose. Besides offering an extra layer of warmth at the hem around the ankles on cold winter days, they added an exciting touch of color and charm. These embroidered borders, or bands, were often made so they could be removed when the skirt itself was worn out and then resewn to a new skirt. Such treasured pieces were often passed from sister to sister, or perhaps from one generation to another.

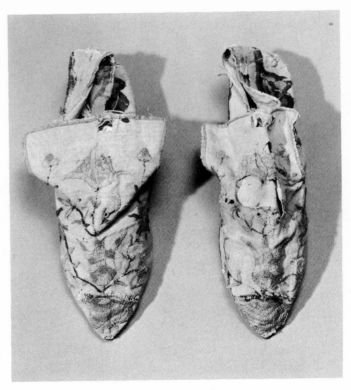

Nightcaps, such as this one from Boston, and a pair of slippers were other items often decorated with embroidery.

Dating from the eighteenth century, a girl's linen dress is embroidered with floral sprays in polychrome crewels.

Elizabeth Bull of Boston made this embroidered white silk dress in 1731.

Courtesy National Index of Design, National Gallery

The embroidered linen waist and skirt breadth was a part of the wedding gown of Mary Meyers of Lebanon, Connecticut, made for her marriage to John Johnson in 1732. The bride spun and wove the linen for her dress.

Courtesy The Wadsworth Atheneum

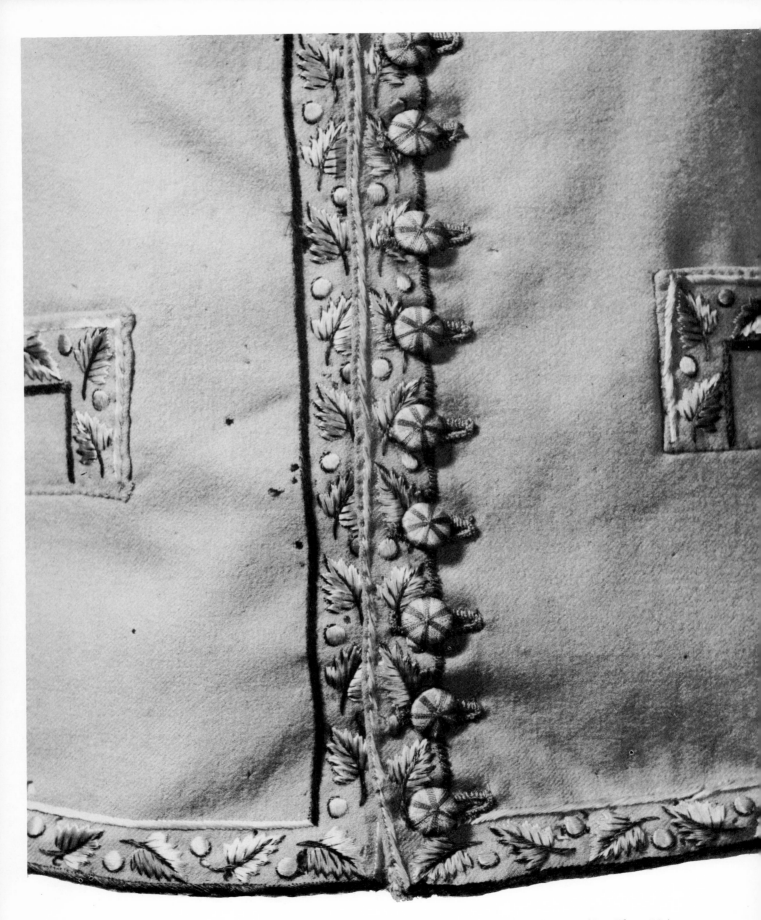

Covered buttons and an embroidered border are features of a man's waistcoat. (See Plate 12.)

Courtesy The Valentine Museum, Richmond, Virginia

Courtesy Museum of Fine Arts, Boston, Gift of Mr. Samuel Cabot

The border of this linen petticoat from Vermont was embroidered in crewels in the late eighteenth century.

Pages 121 - 123.
This embroidered linen skirt features a variety of floral motifs, some of which have been reproduced in detail here, along with other motifs from eighteenth-century pieces, in many museum collections. The skirt is believed to have been part of a gown embroidered by Judith Hale, who was born in 1711 and married John Eaton of Haverhill, Massachusetts.

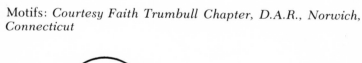

Motifs: *Courtesy Faith Trumbull Chapter, D.A.R., Norwich, Connecticut*

Courtesy The Metropolitan Museum of Art, Rogers Fund, 1942

121

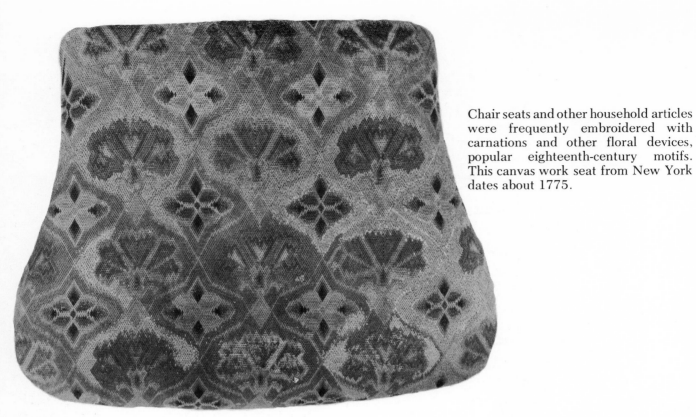

Chair seats and other household articles were frequently embroidered with carnations and other floral devices, popular eighteenth-century motifs. This canvas work seat from New York dates about 1775.

Courtesy Museum of the City of New York

Courtesy Heritage Foundation, Deerfield, Massachusetts

Large floral motifs are worked on a canvas background for this eighteenth-century American chair seat.

Two linen chair seats, showing margins where the design is partly finished, were worked with crewels. The background is filled with stitches, creating an illusion of canvas work.

Courtesy Museum of Fine Arts, Boston, Gift of Mr. and Mrs. Henry K. Metcalf

CANVAS WORK

Canvas work was used in early America for a variety of items, some examples of which are pictured here and others in the section on pictorial needlework. One of the earliest forms of embroidery, it has been traced back to the fourth century A.D. As its name suggests, it is the application of stitches onto a canvas background. Both the design itself and the background areas are usually completely filled. During colonial times this technique was often known in newspaper advertisements as "tent stitch." Later "needlepoint" came into popular use, while today "canvas work" is the preferred term.

Canvas work was not as popular in colonial America as crewelwork and other types of embroidery in which open backgrounds were acceptable. The fact that a greater quantity of yarn was required undoubtedly had some effect upon its popularity. There is little evidence that this technique was widely used for large projects such as bed furnishings. It was, however, often used in the making of smaller pieces such as chair seats, coats of arms, pictures, pocketbooks, and slippers, to mention a few. The most popular stitches were tent, cross, and Roumanian.

125

Green, yellow-brown, pink and white crewels in a "flame-stitch" pattern are embroidered on a pocketbook with cords and pompoms (1790-1810).

Courtesy Henry Francis du Pont Winterthur Museum

The exquisitely embroidered American eighteenth-century doublet is from the collection at Deerfield. It is worked with gold silk thread on a white background.

Courtesy Heritage Foundation, Deerfield, Massachusetts

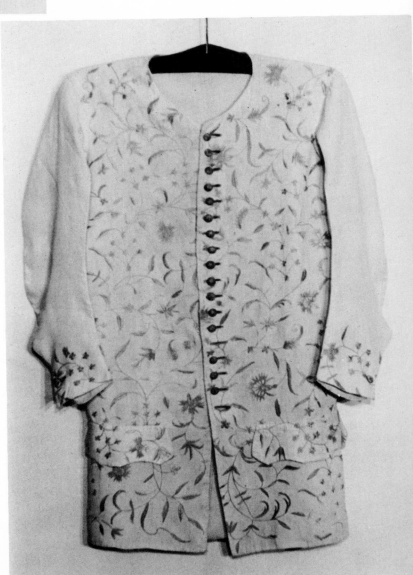

126

Canvas work slippers, once belonging to Maria Sanford Hayden (1790 - 1857), wife of New York Mayor Jeremiah Hayden, were made by working the design through canvas onto black woolen twill. Then the canvas was removed, leaving the embroidery on the background.

Courtesy The Valentine Museum, Richmond, Virginia

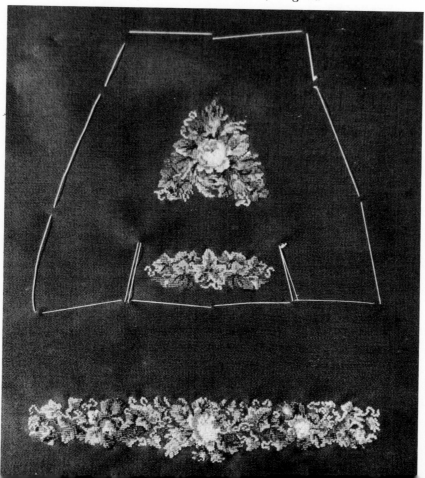

*Courtesy Faith Trumbull Chapter,
D.A.R., Norwich, Connecticut*

The initials "M W" and the date "1761" are incorporated near the top of an embroidered linen pocket *(left)*. An eighteenth-century pocketbook *(above)* features a floral design on canvas, a leaf motif on the flap, and a carnation motif on the body of the purse.

*Courtesy Henry Francis du Pont
Winterthur Museum*

POCKETS AND POCKETBOOKS

Pocketbooks and pockets were popular accessories in an eighteenth-century wardrobe. Embroidery designs for them were often floral, with individual motifs connected by gracefully flowing vines. Some were made in canvas work. Pocketbooks, used by men and sometimes by women, were frequently worked on canvas with backgrounds usually filled with a Florentine (Bargello) stitch design, or with geometric or floral motifs. It is be-

lieved these items were used by their owners on special occasions and exhibited with great pride. Pockets were feminine accessories. They were worn under the skirt and held in place by strings tied around the waist. Access to them was through slits in the skirt and petticoat. They were used to carry keys, coins, small personal treasures, and an assortment of miscellany.

below

White stitches on a dark ground accentuate flowing tendrils of this pocket design, dating from the early to mid-nineteenth century.

Courtesy New Haven Colony Historical Society

129

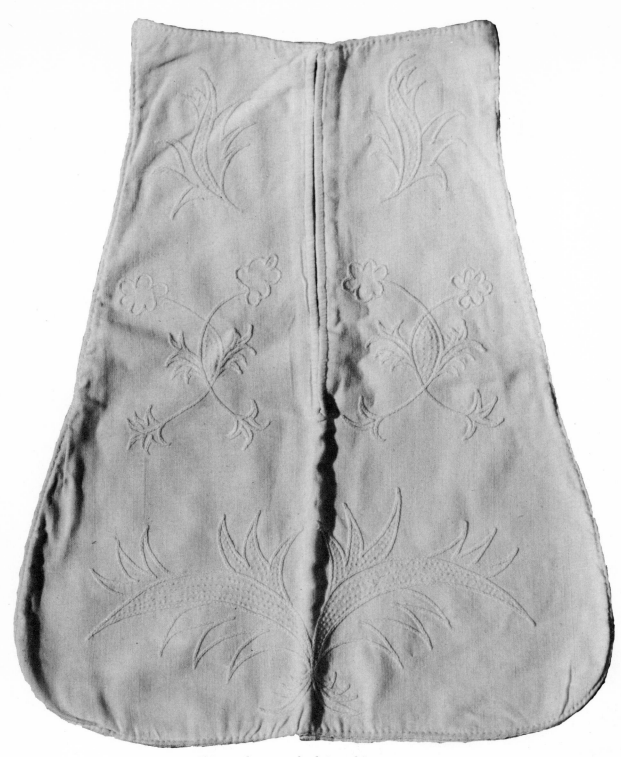

This pocket, worked in white cotton thread on white linen, features leaf motifs. It dates from the early to mid-nineteenth century.

Courtesy New Haven Colony Historical Society

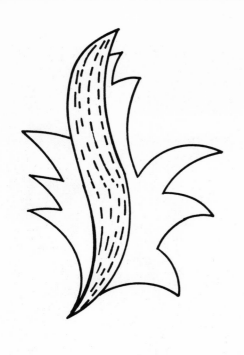

131

Worked in petit point on canvas, a hatchment from Boston (1740-1760) includes a scrolled escutcheon, double coat of arms, and a banner inscribed "Simpkins and Symmes."

Courtesy Henry Francis du Pont Winterthur Museum

CHAPTER THREE

✾ PICTORIAL NEEDLEWORK

Pictures, coats of arms and hatchments, scenic samplers, memorial pieces, maps, and so on provide many examples of picturesque needlework. How better to preserve favorite scenes or mottoes, pleasurable memories, tributes to departed loved ones, needlework themes from the past or ones to be preserved for the future?

Most pictures were worked on canvas, with stitches filling the entire area. Now and then particular stitches were used to accentuate certain elements, such as French knots to suggest the woolly texture of a lamb's fleece. There was no end of subjects — a man sitting beneath a tree with his dog nearby, the famous "Fishing Lady," biblical characters, a hunting scene, landscapes, a bouquet of flowers, a ship, maps, and houses. Pictures were small enough that the embroiderer could often afford the extravagance of filling the background with her stitchery. Frequently pictures bear the initials of the embroiderer, the date it was finished, or perhaps her birth date. Coats of arms were heraldic symbols of family status. Hatchments were square or lozenge-shaped panels bearing the coat of arms of a man who had just died. As funeral devices they were displayed in various manners, at the home, on the coffin, in church, or elsewhere as custom decreed. Several interesting examples are shown here.

The word "sampler" often evokes an image of a neat square or rectangle filled with orderly rows of stitches interspersed by the alphabet, a line or two of numerals, perhaps a verse, the maker's name, age, or birth date, the whole framed by a border as complex as the maker's skill allowed.

There are charming exceptions, some of which are shown here. Early in the 1700's samplers with pictorial overtones appeared, and increased steadily in number as the years went by. A variety of pictorial elements have been identified in eighteenth-century samplers:* angels, birds (flying in cages, trees, or dovecotes), flower beds, houses with and without terraces, pastoral scenes, prominent buildings, stagecoaches, and so on. During and after the American Revolution the list includes Continental soldiers and eagles in majestic postures.

Other pictorial needlework includes maps, although they are not found in any great number.

---

*Three samplers, one dated 1828, one about 1830, and the other about 1834, are shown. Although dated after the Early American era, they are in the tradition of that period.

Courtesy Henry Francis du Pont Winterthur Museum

This needlework picture, made about 1760 by a member of the Stuyvesant family, shows the Nicholas Stuyvesant house in the background.

Courtesy Museum of the City of New York

opposite

The lozenge-shaped hatchment featuring an eagle's head and inscribed "1758. Aet. 15./ Jane Brown," was worked in wool embroidery on wool. It is believed to have been made in Massachusetts.

Four of the Twelve Apostles—Peter, Matthew, Andrew, and Simon the Zealot—are shown in a set of needlework pictures embroidered in silk on satin about 1776-1780 by Prudence Punderson (1758-1784) of Preston, Connecticut.

136

St. Andrew.
He was fastened to a Cross at Patrae.

St. Simon the Zealot.
He was sawed in two. Persia.

St. Bartholomew.
He was Flead alive and then Crucified.

St. Lebbeus.
Whose Surname was Thaddeus.

Also from the set of needlework pictures by Prudence Punderson are the apostles Bartholomew, Lebbeus (Thaddeus), James the Less, and Thomas, with inscriptions giving details of their various martyrdoms.

John the Evangelist, James the Great, Philip, and Judas Iscariot complete the Twelve Apostles needlework pictures by Prudence Punderson.

Courtesy The Connecticut Historical Society

Nautical motifs, rarely found in early American embroidery, are featured in two pieces of pictorial needlework made about 1740.

Courtesy Museum of Fine Arts, Boston, M. and M. Karolik Collection

Embroidered on linen about 1800 in Norwalk, Connecticut, this scenic sampler was originally owned by Sarah Hazelett Raymond.

Courtesy National Index of Design, National Gallery

Sixteen-year-old Mary Batchelder worked this sampler in colored silks on tan linen, progressing from the precision of counted-thread cross-stitches to the beautifully worked vase of flowers and birds.

Courtesy The Cooper-Hewitt Museum of Design

Detailed drawings of the lower motif in the Batchelder sampler are shown *(above)* and a portion of an eighteenth-century Newport sampler *(below)*.

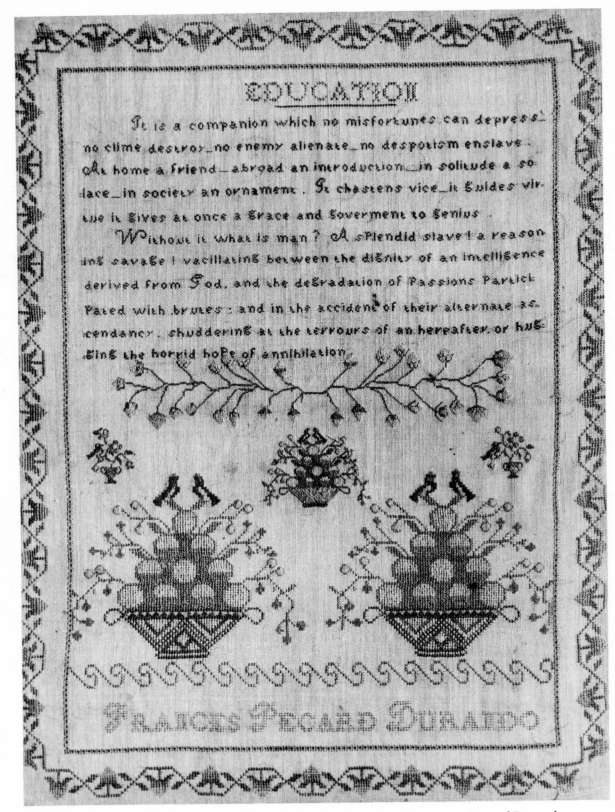

This sampler, entitled "Education," was made about 1830 by Frances Pecard Durando.
Courtesy Museum of the City of New York

Adam and Eve under an apple tree, surrounded by baskets of flowers, are featured in this sampler made by Elizabeth Rowe Terry in 1828. The motifs are worked on linen with colored silks embroidered in cross-stitch and "bird's-eye."

Courtesy The Cooper-Hewitt Museum of Design

Numerals, the alphabet, and a verse prayer were worked by Rebekah Ursula Ousby of Raleigh, North Carolina, in this sampler made about 1834 when she was twelve years old. (See Plate 16.)

Courtesy State Department of Archives and History, Raleigh, North Carolina

Boundaries of continents are embroidered in chenille in the needlework map from
New York State inscribed "Mary M. Franklin / Pleasant Valley / 1808."

Courtesy Henry Francis du Pont Winterthur Museum

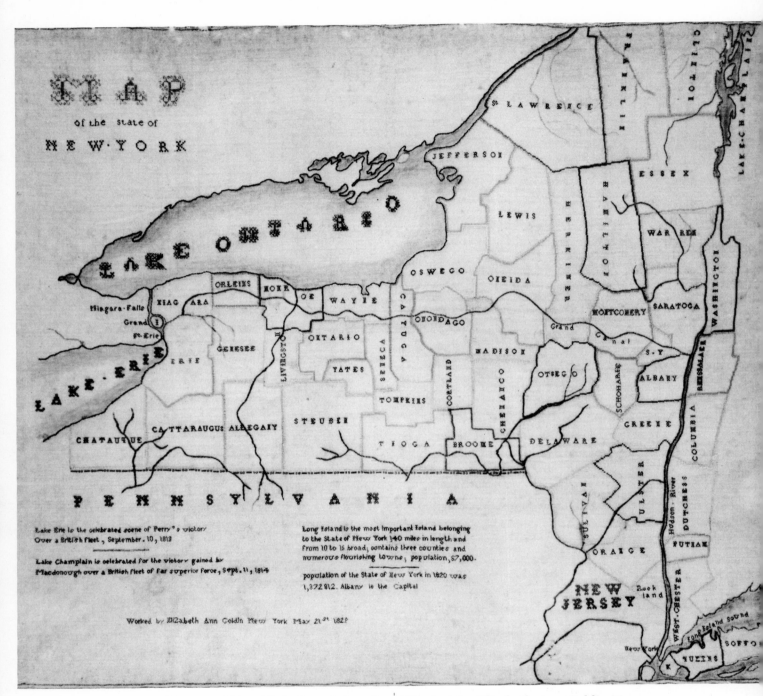

This map of New York State is inscribed "Worked by Elizabeth Ann Goldin New
York May 21st 1822 [9?]."

Courtesy The Cooper-Hewitt Museum of Design

EPILOGUE

At the beginning of the Early American period the colonies were well into the process of defining their economic roles, and were settling into distinctive social patterns, but they had not created artistic identities of their own. As this period ended, economic and social characteristics were well defined, a spectacular political identity had been shaped, and the visual arts were rapidly creating their own forms and traditions. The needle arts were perfected to a degree of excellence that has survived two centuries.

As the Early American period of decorative design flourished during the Age of Enlightenment, so it withered and died during the early years of the Industrial Revolution.

A strange phenomenon attended its passage; a curtain was drawn and it disappeared almost as if it had not existed. Rarely has one century been so oblivious of the attainments of the century immediately preceding it as was the nineteenth century to the esthetic traditions of the eighteenth. The drawn curtain was the Industrial Revolution, and the motivating force was the development of power-driven machines which supplanted human skills.

Textile manufacturing was the first great industry to feel the impact when its newly invented spinning and weaving machines were teamed with steam power. In the great flood of expanding commerce that followed, the artifacts of the eighteenth century were largely forgotten and continued to lie neglected until near the dawn of the twentieth century, when Americans turned from their absorption with the practicalities of the nineteenth century to contemplate once more the esthetic creations of their forebears.

And so the wheel turns toward full circle. What the machine took away it may now return in partial measure at least. It sounded the death knell of the handicraft arts of the eighteenth century. Today it is gradually building a leisured society in which many turn to the arts of their colonial forebears to fill the need to create something beautiful with their own hands.

Thus what is here called "epilogue" should, in a larger sense, be part of an ever-widening prologue to appreciation of the fine craftsmanship, the honest workmanship, the pride of creation, the inherent good taste, and the enduring traditions created and nurtured in colonial America.

APPENDIX

STATE FLOWERS, BIRDS, AND TREES

States in order of union entry.

		FLOWERS	BIRDS	TREES
1787	Del.	peach blossom	blue hen chicken	American holly
1787	Penna.	mountain laurel	ruffed grouse	hemlock
1787	N.J.	purple violet	American goldfinch	red oak
1788	Ga.	Cherokee rose	brown thrasher	live oak
1788	Conn.	mountain laurel	American robin	white oak
1788	Mass.	mayflower	chickadee	American elm
1788	Md.	black-eyed Susan	Baltimore oriole	white oak
1788	S.C.	Carolina (yellow) jessamine	Carolina wren	palmetto
1788	N.H.	purple lilac	purple finch	white birch
1788	Va.	American dogwood	cardinal	American dogwood
1788	N.Y.	rose	eastern bluebird	sugar maple
1789	N.C.	dogwood	cardinal	pine
1790	R.I.	violet	Rhode Island red	maple
1791	Vt.	red clover	hermit thrush	sugar maple
1792	Ky.	goldenrod	cardinal	tulip tree
1796	Tenn.	iris	mockingbird	tulip poplar
1803	Ohio	scarlet carnation	cardinal	Ohio buckeye
1812	La.	southern magnolia	eastern brown pelican	bald cypress
1816	Ind.	peony	cardinal	tulip tree
1817	Miss.	magnolia	mockingbird	magnolia
1818	Ill.	violet	cardinal	oak
1819	Ala.	camellia	yellowhammer	long-leaf pine
1820	Maine	pine cone and tassel	chickadee	white pine
1821	Mo.	hawthorn	eastern bluebird	dogwood

1836	Ark.	apple blossom	mockingbird	short-leaf pine
1837	Mich.	apple blossom	robin	white pine
1845	Fla.	orange blossom	mockingbird	sabal palm
1845	Texas	bluebonnet	mockingbird	pecan
1846	Iowa	wild rose	American goldfinch	oak
1848	Wis.	wood violet	robin	sugar maple
1850	Calif.	golden poppy	valley quail	redwood
1858	Minn.	showy lady's slipper	loon	red (Norway) pine
1859	Oregon	Oregon grape	western meadowlark	Douglas fir
1861	Kansas	sunflower	western meadowlark	cottonwood
1863	West Va.	rhododendron	cardinal	sugar maple
1864	Nevada	sagebrush	mountain bluebird	single-leaf piñon
1867	Nebr.	goldenrod	western meadowlark	American elm
1876	Colo.	columbine	lark bunting	Colorado blue spruce
1889	N.D.	wild prairie rose	western meadowlark	American elm
1889	S.D.	pasque	ring-necked pheasant	Black Hills spruce
1889	Mont.	bitterroot	western meadowlark	ponderosa pine
1889	Wash.	rhododendron	American goldfinch	western hemlock
1890	Idaho	syringa mock orange	mountain bluebird	white pine
1890	Wyo.	Indian paintbrush	western meadowlark	cottonwood
1896	Utah	sego lily	California gull	blue spruce
1907	Okla.	mistletoe	scissor-tailed flycatcher	redbud
1912	N. Mex.	yucca	roadrunner	piñon (nut pine)
1912	Ariz.	giant cactus (or saguaro)	cactus wren	paloverde
1959	Alaska	forget-me-not	willow ptarmigan	Sitka spruce
1959	Hawaii	hibiscus	nene	candlenut
	D.C.	American beauty rose	wood thrush	scarlet oak

BIBLIOGRAPHY

American Folk Art: 1750-1900. The Museum of Modern Art. New York: W. W. Norton & Company, Inc., 1932.

Art of Colouring and Painting Landscapes, The. Baltimore: Fielding Lucas, Jr., 1815.

BAILYN, BERNARD. *The New England Merchants in the Seventeenth Century.* New York: Harper Torchbooks, 1964.

BARKER, VIRGIL. *American Painting.* New York: The Macmillan Company, 1950.

BARTRAM, WILLIAM. *Travels of William Bartram (1773-1778).* New York: Dover Publications, Inc., 1955.

BENSON, MARY SUMNER. *Women in Eighteenth-Century America.* Port Washington, New York: Kennikat Press, Inc., 1966.

BOLTON, ETHEL STANWOOD, and COE, EVA JOHNSTON. *American Samplers.* Boston: The Massachusetts Society of the Colonial Dames of America, 1921.

BOORSTIN, DANIEL J. *The Americans (The Colonial Experience).* New York: Random House, 1958.

BRIDENBAUGH, CARL. *Cities in Revolt: Urban Life in America, 1743-1776.* New York: Capricorn Books, 1964.

————. *Cities in the Wilderness: Urban Life in America, 1625-1742.* New York: Capricorn Books, 1964.

BURROUGHS, ALAN. *Limners and Likenesses.* Cambridge, Massachusetts: Harvard University Press, 1936.

CALHOUN, ARTHUR W. *A Social History of the American Family.* (Vol. I, Colonial Period.) Cleveland: The Arthur H. Clark Company, 1917.

CAPPON, LESTER J., and DUFF, STELLA F. *The Virginia Gazette Index.* 2 vols. Williamsburg: Institute of Early American History and Culture, 1950.

CARMAN, HARRY J., SYRETTE, HAROLD C., and WISHY, BERNARD W. *The History of the American People.* Vol. I. New York: Alfred A. Knopf, 1960.

CAUGHEY, JOHN W., and MAY, ERNEST R. *A History of the United States.* Chicago: Rand McNally & Company, 1964.

CAVALLO, ADOLPH S. "New England Crewel Embroideries," *Connecticut Historical Society Bulletin* (April, 1959).

CHAMBERS, EPHRIAM, F. R. S. *Cyclopaedia: or, an Universal Dictionary of Arts and Sciences.* 4 vols. London: 1791.

CHANNING, GEORGE G. *Early Recollections of Newport, R.I. (1793-1811).* Boston: Nichols and Noyes, 1868.

CHAPMAN, SUZANNE E. *Early American Design Motifs.* New York: Dover Publications, Inc., 1952.

CHITWOOD, OLIVER PERRY. *A History of Colonial America.* New York: Harper & Brothers, 1948.

CHRISTENSEN, ERWIN O. *The Index of American Design.* New York: The Macmillan Company, 1959.

CLOUZOT, HENRI. *Painted and Printed Fabrics: 1760-1815.* New York: Metropolitan Museum of Art, 1927.

COHEN, HENNIG. *The South Carolina Gazette.* Columbia, S.C.: University of South Carolina Press, 1953.

COLBY, AVERIL. *Samplers.* London: B. T. Batsford Ltd., 1964.

CRAGIE, SIR WILLIAM A., and HULBERT, JAMES R. (eds.). *A Dictionary of American English on Historical Principles.* 4 vols. Chicago: The University of Chicago Press, 1938.

CRAIG, JAMES H. *The Arts and Crafts in North Carolina.* Winston-Salem: The Museum of Early Southern Decorative Arts, 1965.

CUMMINGS, ABBOTT LOWELL. *Bed Hangings.* Boston: The Society for the Preservation of New England Antiquities, 1961.

———(ed.). *Rural Household Inventories: 1675 - 1775.* Boston: The Society for the Preservation of New England Antiquities, 1964.

DOW, GEORGE FRANCIS. *Arts and Crafts in New England.* Topsfield, Massachusetts: The Wayside Press, 1927.

DREPPARD, CARL W. *American Drawing Books.* New York: New York Public Library, 1946.

DUNLAP, WILLIAM. *The Arts of Design in the United States.* 3 vols. Boston: C. E. Goodspeed & Company, 1918.

EARLE, ALICE MORSE. *Child Life in Colonial Days.* New York: The Macmillan Company, 1929.

———. *Home Life in Colonial Days.* New York: Grosset & Dunlap, 1907.

———. *Two Centuries of Costume in America.* 2 vols. New York: The Macmillan Company, 1903.

Elements of Drawing, The. New York: John Low, 1804.

Encyclopaedia Britannica, 1966 edition, 24 vols.

Encyclopedia Americana, International Edition, 1966. 30 vols.

FISKE, JOHN. *The Beginnings of New England.* New York and Boston: Houghton Mifflin Company, 1898.

———. *The Dutch and Quaker Colonies in America.* 2 vols. New York and Boston: Houghton Mifflin Company, 1903.

FLEXNER, JAMES THOMAS. *The First Flowers of Our Wilderness.* Boston: Houghton Mifflin Company, 1947.

FORD, ALICE. *Pictorial Folk Art—New England to California.* New York and London: The Studio Publications, Inc., 1949.

FRIIS, HERMAN R. "Population Maps of the Colonies and the United States: 1625 - 1790," *Bulletin #3 of the American Geographical Society* (New York, 1940).

GOTTESMAN, RITA. *The Arts and Crafts in New York.* New York: New-York Historical Society, 1938.

HALSEY, R. T. H., and TOWER, ELIZABETH. *The Homes of Our Ancestors.* New York: Doubleday, Page, and Company, 1925.

HANSEN, MARCUS LEE. *The Atlantic Migration: 1607 - 1860.* New York: Harper Torchbooks, 1961.

HARBESON, GEORGIANA BROWN. *American Needlework.* New York: Bonanza Books, 1961.

HIPKISS, EDWIN J. *Eighteenth-Century American Arts.* Cambridge, Massachusetts: Harvard University Press, 1941.

HUNTER, GEORGE LELAND. *Decorative Textiles.* Philadelphia: J. B. Lippincott Company, 1918.

JEFFERSON, THOMAS. *Notes on the State of Virginia.* New York: Harper Torchbooks, 1964.

JERNEGAN, MARCUS WILSON. *The American Colonies.* New York: Longmans, Green and Company, 1929.

JOHNSON, CLIFTON. *Old-Time Schools and School-Books.* New York: Dover Publications, Inc., 1963.

JONES, HOWARD MUMFORD. *O Strange New World.* New York: The Viking Press, 1964.

KALM, PETER. *Travels in North America (1750).* 2 vols. New York: Dover Publications, Inc., 1966.

KAUFFMAN, HENRY J. *Pennsylvania Dutch American Folk Art.* New York: Dover Publications, Inc., 1964.

KIEFER, MONICA. *American Children Through Their Books: 1730 - 1835.* Philadelphia: University of Pennsylvania Press, 1948.

KING, BUCKY. *Creative Canvas Embroidery.* New York: Hearthside Press, Inc., 1963.

Lady's Book, The. Philadelphia: L. A. Godey & Company, 1830.

LIPMAN, JEAN, and WINCHESTER, ALICE. *Primitive Painters in America.* New York: Dodd, Mead & Company, 1950.

LITTLE, FRANCES. *Early American Textiles.* New York: The Century Company, 1931.

LITTLE, NINA FLETCHER. *The Abby Aldrich Rockefeller Folk Art Collection.* Boston: Little, Brown and Company, 1957.

MCCLELLAN, ELIZABETH. *History of American Costume: 1607 - 1870.* New York: Tudor Publishing Company, 1937.

MCCLELLAND, NANCY. *Historic Wall-Papers.* Philadelphia: J. B. Lippincott Company, 1924.

MIDDLEKAUFF, ROBERT. *Ancients and Axioms: Secondary Education in Eighteenth-Century New England.* New Haven: Yale University Press. 1963.

MORGAN, EDMUND S. *Virginians at Home: Family Life in the Eighteenth Century.* New York: Holt, Rinehart & Winston, 1959.

MORISON, SAMUEL ELIOT. *The Oxford History of the American People.* New York: Oxford University Press, 1965.

MORSE, JEDIDIAH. *The American Universal Geography.* 2 vols. Boston: Isaiah Thomas & Ebenezer T. Andrews, 1793.

MOTT, FRANK LUTHER. *American Journalism.* New York: The Macmillan Company, 1941.

———. *A History of American Magazines* (Vol. I, 1741 - 1850). New York: D. Appleton and Company, 1930.

NORTHEND, MARY H. *Colonial Homes and Their Furnishings.* Boston: Little, Brown and Company, 1912.

NYE, RUSSEL BLAINE. *The Cultural Life of the New Nation*

(1776 - 1830). New York: Harper Torchbooks, 1963.

One Thousand Valuable Secrets, in the Elegant and Useful Arts. Philadelphia: B. Davies & T. Stephens, 1795.

PAYNE, BLANCHE. *History of Costume.* New York: Harper & Row, 1965.

PIERCY, JOSEPHINE K. *Anne Bradstreet.* New York: Twayne Publishers, 1965.

PRIME, ALFRED COXE. *The Arts and Crafts in Philadelphia, Maryland and South Carolina.* Philadelphia: The Walpole Society, 1929.

RANDOLPH, SARAH N. *The Domestic Life of Thomas Jefferson.* Cambridge, Massachusetts: Harvard University Press, 1939.

RICHARDSON, E. P. *Painting in America.* New York: Thomas Y. Crowell Company, 1956.

ROBERTSON, ARCHIBALD. *Elements of the Graphic Arts.* New York: David Longworth, 1802.

SANBORN, KATE. *Old Time Wall Papers.* New York: The Literary Collector Press, 1905.

SCHUETTE, MARIE, and MÜLLER-CHRISTENSEN, SIGRID. *A Pictorial History of Embroidery.* New York: Frederick A. Praeger, 1964.

SMALL, WALTER SCOTT. *Early New England Schools.* Boston: Ginn and Company, 1914.

SPRUILL, JULIA CHERRY. *Women's Life and Work in the Southern Colonies.* Chapel Hill, N.C.: University of North Carolina Press, 1938.

STEARNS, BERTHA M. "Early New England Magazines for Ladies," *New England Quarterly* (January - October, 1929).

SWEM, E. G. *Brothers of the Spade.* Barre, Massachusetts: Barre Gazette, 1957.

TASSIN, ALGERNON. *The Magazine in America.* New York: Dodd, Mead and Company, 1916.

TAYLOR, RAYMOND L. *Plants of Colonial Days.* Williamsburg: Colonial Williamsburg, 1952.

TOWNSEND, GERTRUDE. "Introduction to the Study of 18th-Century New England Embroidery," *Bulletin of the Museum of Fine Arts* (Boston, April, 1941).

WEBSTER, NOAH. *A Compendious Dictionary of the English Language.* Hartford: Hudson & Goodwin, 1806.

WERTENBAKER, THOMAS J. *The Golden Age of Colonial Culture.* Ithaca, N.Y.: Cornell University Press, 1959.

WHEELER, CANDACE. *The Development of Embroidery in America.* New York: Harper & Brothers, 1921.

WHITEHILL, WATER MUIR, and GARRETT, WENDELL D. and JANE N. *The Arts in Early American History.* Williamsburg: Institute of Early American History and Culture, 1965.

WHITMORE, WILLIAM H. *Notes Concerning Peter Pelham.* Cambridge, Massachusetts: John Wilson and Son, 1867.

WILCOX, R. TURNER. *Five Centuries of American Costume.* New York: Charles Scribner's Sons, 1963.

WILLIAMS, JOHN ROGERS (ed.). *Philip Vickers Fithian Journal and Letters: 1767 - 1774.* Princeton, N.J.: Princeton Historical Association, 1900.

WILLICH, A. F. M. *The Domestic Encyclopedia.* 5 vols. Philadelphia: Birch and Small, 1803 - 1804.

WILSON, ALEXANDER. *American Ornithology.* 9 vols. Philadelphia: Bradford and Inskeep, 1808 - 1815.

WRIGHT, LOUIS B. *The Cultural Life of the American Colonies (1607 - 1763).* New York: Harper Torchbooks, 1962.

INDEX

A

Accessories, 117-32
Apostles, 136-41
Apparel, 117-32
Appliqué, 53, 72, 73, 94-104
Apron, pocketed, 116

B

Bases, 37
Bed
 covers (coverlets), 38, 48-52, 60-61, 63,
  64, 65, 71, 72, 73, 74, 75, 84, 85, 86,
  87, 88, 95, 96-98, 99-101, 102-104, 105,
  106-107, 108-109, 110, 111, 112, 113,
  114, 115

 furnishings, 37-116
 hangings, 20, 45, 54, 71
 rugs, 112-15
 valances, 38-39, 54, 60, 81, 82-83
  patterns, 24
Bedroom, Benkard, 20
Benkard memorial bedroom, 20
Birds, state, 152-53
Borders, floral, 58
Brocade patterns, 29
Button coverings, 76
Buttonhole stitch, 56

C

Canvas work, 78, 124-27, 128, 132, 133
Chain stitch, 12, 56
Chair seats, 78, 124, 125

Coats of arms, 132, 133
Colonial
    interior, 20
    magazines, 28
    newspapers, 28
    society, 17
Cotton threads, 22
Counterpanes, 38, 111; *also see* Bed covers
Coverlets, *see* Bed covers
Crewels, 39, 48, 54, 61, 63, 66, 67, 75, 76,
    77, 81, 86, 114, 116, 118, 121, 125, 126
Cross stitch, 56, 125, 144, 147
Curtains (hangings), 37, 57

D

Damask pattern, 29
Design
    notebooks, 21, 26
    traditions, 13, 18, 19
Doublet, 126
Drawing, 23
Drawn fabric work, 105, 108-109, 111
Drawn thread, 105
Dress border, pattern, 24
Dresses, 76, 118, 119
    design, 21
Dust ruffles, 38

E

Egyptian hanging, 12
European decorative influences, 15, 17, 18, 29

F

Fabrics, patterned, 28-29
Feather stitch, 56
Fishbone stitch, 56
"Flame-stitch" pattern, 126
Floral
    borders, 58, 73
    designs, 33, 36-47, 55, 56-88
Florentine (Bargello) stitch, 128
Flounces, 37
Flowers, state, 152-53
French knots, 56, 133
Funeral devices, 133

G

"Garden coverlet," 106-107
Godey's Lady's Book, 28

H

Hancock, John, family, 52, 65
Hangings, *see* Bed hangings; Curtains
Hatchments, 132, 133, 134
Head cloths, 38, 53
Herringbone stitch, 56

I

Imported embroideries, 30
India prints, 73, 102-104
Instruction, needlework, 23, 25-26, 32, 33
Itinerant artists, 30, 35

L

Lady's Magazine, The, 16, 26

M

Magazines, colonial, 28
Maps, 149, 150
Memorial pieces, 9
Metal threads, 78
Mountmellick, 105

N

Nautical motifs, 84, 142
Newspapers, colonial, 28
    announcements, 17, 18, 26, 36
Nightcaps, 118
Notebooks, design, 21
Notices, 36

O

Outline stitch, 56

P

Painted fabrics, 29
Panels, 57, 84-85
Paper hangings, 29-30
Parchment pattern, 27
Patchwork quilts, 89
Pattern books, 26
Patterned fabrics, 28-29
Patterns, 16, 18, 27
  brocade, 29
  damask, 29
  paper, 24
  parchment, 27
  published, 16, 26, 28
Pelham, Peter, 30, 35
Petit point, 132
Petticoat borders, 24, 77, 117, 121
Pictorial needlework, 20, 78, 79, 133-50
Pocketbooks, 126, 128
Pockets, 77, 128, 129, 130
Portraitists, 30, 31, 35
Printed fabrics, 29
Published patterns, 26, 28

Q

Quilts, 42, 62, 89-93

R

Robertson, Archibald, 30
Roumanian stitch, 56, 125

S

Samplers, 9, 22-23, 33, 34, 80, 133-34, 143,
      144, 145, 146, 147, 148
Satin stitch, 56
Schools, 23, 25-26, 32
Seats, chair, 78, 124, 125
Seed stitch, 56
Shoes, patterns, 16
Silk embroidery, 22, 34, 61, 76, 78, 79
Skirt, 121
Slippers, 118, 127
Sprigs, patterns, 16

State
  birds, 152-53
  flowers, 152-53
  trees, 152-53
Stitches, 12
  buttonhole, 56
  chain, 12, 56
  cross, 56, 125, 144, 147
  feather, 56
  fishbone, 56
  Florentine (Bargello), 128
  French knots, 56, 133
  herringbone, 56
  outline, 56
  Roumanian, 56, 125
  satin, 56
  seed, 56
  straight, 56
  surface, 71, 105
  tent, 125
"Story coverlet," 73, 102-104
Straight stitch, 56
Stuart, Gilbert, 31
"Stuffed work," 106-107
Surface stitch, 71, 105

T

Table cover, 74, 88
Teachers, 23, 25-26
Teaching samplers, 34, 80
"Tent stitch," 125
Tester, 38, 53
Threads, 22, 78, 112
Trees, state, 152-53

V

Valances (vallens), 37, 38-39, 54, 59, 60, 81, 82-83, 116;
      also see Bed valances
  patterns, 24

W

Waistcoats, 30, 76, 120
Wallpaper, 29-30
Wedding gown, 119
White work, 105-111
Women's roles, 18
Wool threads, 22, 78, 112

O   c.1
746.44
D

Davis, Mildred J.

Early American embroidery

designs

MR
1219